KT-498-159

why HEADLESS CHICKENS run

and OTHER BONKERS things you need to KNOW

WRITTEN by

Michael Cox

Illustrated by Clive Goddard

SCHOLASTIC

Scholastic Children's Books,
Euston House, 24 Eversholt Street,
London, NW1 1DB, UK

A division of Scholastic Ltd
London ~ New York ~ Toronto ~ Sydney ~ Auckland
Mexico City ~ New Delhi ~ Hong Kong

First published in the UK by Scholastic Ltd, 2010

Text copyright © Michael Cox, 2010
Illustration copyright © Clive Goddard, 2010
All rights reserved

ISBN 978 1407 11649 5

Printed and bound in the UK by CPI Mackays, Chatham ME5 8TD

2 4 6 8 10 9 7 5 3 1

The BRILLIANTLY bonkers book of everything (apart from the BITS that aren't in it)

HOW many loaves of bread you'll EAT, **dreams** you'll dream and **TOILET ROLLS** you'll use during your **LIFE**...

→ INTRODUCTION

This book is full to bursting with stories and facts that are so **completely bonkers**, weird and astounding that you could well be forgiven for thinking they aren't true.

For instance, there's the utterly astonishing story of a chicken called Mike who walked around without his head for eighteen whole months. And then there's the really daft bit about the batty boffin who not only had himself roasted alive in an oven to 'see what would happen', but also had himself lowered into an active volcano. There's also the tale of the bonkers Yorkshire farmer who liked to go fox hunting on his pet bull, not with foxhounds, but accompanied by his pack of pet pigs! And there's a rather sickening saga of a dotty doctor who encouraged his patients to puke straight into his own mouth! All of which are totally true! As is everything else in this collection of all things amazing and out-of-this-world. So if you want to find out all sorts of completely bonkers and astounding true stuff such as ...

☞ HOW to hypnotize an alligator

☞ WHAT objects hundreds of children get stuck up their noses every year

---

☞ WHO had all the cows on his country estate stencilled with a pretty pattern because he thought it would make them 'look nicer'

☞ WHICH schoolboy was whipped for not smoking at breakfast

☞ WHAT a 'snollygoster' is

☞ **HOW** to get fired out of a cannon, ride a wild bull, get attacked by a shark and live to tell the tale

☞ **WHICH** frog deliberately breaks its own bones to produce instant claws whenever it feels threatened

☞ **WHO** took 55 years to finish his Olympic marathon run

☞ **HOW** many loaves of bread you'll eat, dreams you'll dream and toilet rolls you'll use during your life...

...plus loads more stuff about us very weird creatures known as human beings, as well as the rest of the animal world, then this is the book for you! So what are you waiting for? Dive in and get completely flabbersmacked, gobghasted and possibly even bogglewildered!

FIVE BONKERS INVENTIONS ✈

The baby CAGE

If you lived in posh Chelsea in the 1930s and had a baby but
no garden, you bought a baby cage. Not to put your baby in
if it misbehaved, but to allow it to get some fresh air. You
simply attached the wire cage to the outside of your
apartment window, bunged the baby in it and left it to coo
and gurgle several storeys above the street below.

PITH-HELMET water reservoir

This hat was invented in the 1890s to help German soldiers
who often went thirsty in tropical Africa due to lack of water.
Any rain that did fall was caught in the hat's built-in basin
which also had its own tap. The hat was actually used by
the soldiers but then abandoned when they began suffering
from the horrible disease known as dysentery. The inventor
hadn't taken into account that amoebae and other sorts of
nasties would thrive in the reservoir, making its contents
unfit for drinking.

The ANTI-GARROTING collar

Victorian London was a dangerous place where pairs of thieves known as 'garrotters' would mug you at the drop of a top hat. While one seized you by the throat and throttled or 'garroted' you, the other would steal your valuables.

But not if you were wearing your anti-garroting collar! This was quite simply a leather band with metal spikes on it, which you wore under your scarf or coat's high-collar. The moment the thief grabbed you by the neck the spikes would sink into his hands. But of course you had to be very careful not to put your anti-garroting collar on inside-out.

The Japanese baby MOP

These aren't for mopping babies. They're for mopping and polishing floors.

And it's the baby who does the mopping! Simply attach the mop to your baby, then, as it crawls happily round your wooden and tile floors, it mops them. When your baby learns to walk you simply buy it a pair of floor-mopping bootees.

'UNDER-EASE' airtight underwear

These underpants are made from air-tight fabric and completely sealed with elastic around the waistband and legs. They also have a replaceable charcoal filter that removes bad-smelling gases before they escape. In other words, you wear them to stop other people from detecting the obnoxious odour of your waste gases (or 'raspberry tarts', as they're known by gastroenterologists). The advertising slogan urges you to 'Wear them for the ones you love'. Which is all fine, but what happens when you take them off?

GONE WITH THE WIND

Five fearsome facts about flatulence which might just ... blow you away!

1 All of us (including, believe it or not, Queen Elizabeth II, David Beckham and that bloke who reads the 6 o'clock news) blast out about 14 botty-burps a day, which amounts to one-and-a-half litres of pongy, and not so pongy, gas. In other words enough to blow up a balloon (party sort, not hot air!). Which all adds up to a dizzying 35,815 litres of the stuff in a lifetime.

2 Farts are gas which is produced by our digestive process. As the bacteria in our large intestine break down food, it causes it to ferment. This produces nitrogen, carbon dioxide, hydrogen, methane and hydrogen sulphide. Some of these gases are absorbed back into our body but the rest are expelled through our bottom.

3 Just as the 16th-century Earl of Oxford was in the middle of bowing to Queen Elizabeth I, he accidentally let out a very loud botty-burp. The Earl was so embarrassed and ashamed about his little 'slip-up' that he actually left the country for seven years! When he did eventually return to England and the royal palace, the Queen said to him, 'You are welcome back to court, my Lord. Fear not, we have forgot the fart.'

4 When he was a child, Frenchman Joseph Pujol discovered that he could suck large amounts of water into his bottom then squirt it out over a distance of several metres. On growing up, Joseph adopted the stage name, Le Petomane (don't ask!), and began to make his living with his amazingly versatile behind. He amused and entertained huge audiences, including famous people of his day such as Sigmund Freud and the Prince of Wales (who ought to have known better).

The highlights of Joseph's show included...

a) Imitating the sound of cannon fire and thunderstorms.

b) Farting an impression of the Great San Francisco Earthquake.

c) Blowing out a candle from several metres away.

d) Making the sound of a dressmaker ripping 2 metres of calico cotton. This particular sound effect was created by just one fart which lasted an astonishing ten seconds.

e) Smoking a cigarette from a tube inserted into his bottom.

f) Playing a flute from the same tube.

5 In August 1977 a vet in Holland was called out to treat a cow with a stomach upset. In order to investigate the problem he inserted a tube into the cow's bottom. Then he struck a match. This was not a good idea. A moment later a great jet of flame whooshed out of the cow's backside, first setting some bales of straw on fire and then the entire farm. The vet was fined £140 ... for arson!

Fortunately, we **never expel** so much WIND in one go that it does actually send us hurtling into space. However, if you would like to '**go ballistic**', why not try the first of OUR...

Something BONKERS to do on a Boring Sunday Afternoon

Go completely ballistic!

How to be a human cannonball

Important note:

You have be of a certain 'calibre' to become a human cannonball (groan). Among the qualities you must possess if you are seriously considering being blasted out of an enormous gun barrel and flying through the air at speeds of up to 90 mph are: courage, strength, concentration, a grasp of basic maths and physics but, most importantly of all, limitless stupidity. Prepared to give it a 'shot'? OK! It's time to bite the bullet. No, sorry, it's time to be the bullet!

First the good news: you aren't going to be blasted from the cannon with gunpowder. You'll be propelled skyward by a jet of compressed air. The bang, smoke, flash and sparks are created by fireworks.

Now the bad news: out of the fifty or so human cannonballs in history, thirty of them have been killed by 'work-related injuries'. Still keen? OK (young imbecile), here's what to do…

1 Get fit. And if you're overweight, get slim. What could be more embarrassing than, post-blast, finding that you're still in the barrel of your cannon, hopelessly jammed, because of all your extra pounds. At Battersea, London, in 1977, the bikini-clad, human cannonball known as Miss Rita Thunderbird remained jammed in the barrel of her cannon after the 'big bang'. However, just moments later, spectators were amazed to see her bra go soaring over the River Thames.

2 Get yourself a 'flash-bang-wallop' new name. Something like the Flying Fury, Miss Missile or The Pocket-Rocket, but definitely not Colin the Custard Pie.

3 Apply for the job of human cannonball. Most vacancies can be found at circuses and fairs. Definitely avoid battlefields and war-zones.

4 Get a dummy. No, not that sort of dummy!

NB: If you're going to do this properly, your dummy should match your own weight and proportions.

5 Practice firing the 'pretend you' out of the cannon in order to plan your path through the air. You do this by making lots of calculations involving your weight, the force at which you will be blasted and where you hope to land. The last bit is most important of all. You will be aiming, quite literally, to flop down on some nice comfy airbags or a safety net.

6 OK, it's time for you to 'go ballistic'. But first, another warning. Try to avoid being blasted on a windy day as it is highly likely that you will be blown off course.

7 Wearing a suitably heroic-looking outfit and crash-helmet, stride heroically to your cannon.

Important style note:

No matter how terrified you're feeling, you must resist the temptation to wet yourself while you're doing this, as it will detract somewhat from your heroic, devil-may-care image.

8 Mount the ladder and lower yourself into the hollow, topless cylinder which will now slide back down the cannon in readiness for being 'blasted' by the compressed air. The air will push the cylinder up the barrel but then it will stop at the top. However, you … will keep going.

9 You are about to fly through the air for 200 feet at a maximum height of 100 feet whilst accelerating at 12Gs (12 times the force of gravity). That's similar to the force experienced by fighter pilots as they make a turn. Whilst flying, you must remember to keep your body completely stiff and straight until the moment before you hit the net or airbags. At this point, you must flip your body over so that you land on your back. Perfect timing is essential! Flip too soon and you miss your soft landing. Turn too late and you land on your head, possibly breaking your back or neck.

10 Warning: At this point it's only fair to tell you that many human cannonballs actually blackout while they're flying through the air. Being completely unconscious will of course put you at something of a disadvantage as you attempt to carry out the above actions. Don't say you weren't warned!

FINAL TIP:

If you lose your nerve at the last minute, you could always sneakily replace yourself with your dummy and hope your audience doesn't notice.

One human cannonball lost his nerve and it cost him his job. Not because he was afraid of being shot out of the cannon. It was because, believe it or not, he was afraid of flying! His employers wanted him to fly to a space centre in Brazil where he would train in dealing with G forces. He refused, so they, err, fired him!

Early human cannonballs were propelled by giant springs built into a 'lookalike' cannon, all of which was no doubt dreamed up by a highly imaginative, but slightly bonkers inventor.

Now, as a **CIRCUS** ringmaster might say, 'HERE for your AMAZEMENT, amusement and enlightenment are some more **inventions** – some slightly **Bonkers**, and others completely BONKERS!'

The FLAMETHROWER car

If you are the victim of an attempted car-jacking, don't worry. Simply press the extra pedal on the floor of your 'Blaster' car and flames will leap from your car's front doors, instantly barbecuing any would-be thieves. On sale in South Africa where there are thousands of car-jackings every year.

The CAT-MIAOW machine

This mechanical cat was invented in Japan in 1963 to scare off mice and rats. It meowed ten times a minute and the eyes lit up each time it did (but it was later beaten to death by a gang of mechanical rats).

The completely circular BATTLE ship

Named the POPOVKA after Admiral Popov, the Russian who designed it in 1873. Despite having its six enormous engines going at full speed, the POPOVKA could only travel at 6 mph. This was slower than the current of the river on which these saucer-shaped ships were tested, so not only were they instantly swept out to sea, but they twizzled around and around, making their sailors really sea-sick. When the crew tried to fire the guns, their recoil also caused the ship to rotate, so the guns were no longer pointing at the target. Now you know why you see so few circular ships.

The wheeled alarm clock

Clocky is an alarm clock that runs away and hides if you don't get out of bed. All right, you can switch him off the first time he beeps. But if you still stay in bed, the next time he sounds, he jumps off the bedside table and 'runs' away, beeping constantly. So you have to get out of bed in order to switch off the irritating little blighter. This wheely bright idea should be a 'runaway' success!

The Analytical Engine

This hugely complicated machine was the forerunner of all modern computers. It was designed by Charles Babbage, who began working on it in the 1830s and was still twiddling and fiddling with his mechanical computing device right up until his death in 1871. However, Charles's great idea was about 100 years ahead of its time and for various reasons, including a lack of technical know-how, money and materials, it was never actually built. But a model of it was made in 1992. You can see it at the London Science Museum. The great thing about the Analytical Engine was that it punched holes into cards which it later 'read'. This method of inputting computer data was used right up until the latter 20th century.

And where did Charles get his punched card idea from?

Well, in the early 18th century a textile worker in France devised a method of controlling a weaving loom with perforated paper tape. This paper tape was later developed into cards with rows of holes punched in them, each row corresponding to one row of a weaving design. In other words the looms were being 'programmed' to work in a certain way. So, bonkers as it may sound, the centuries-old art of weaving had an enormous impact on the mind-boggling world of computing.

Now, this BOOK wouldn't be complete without featuring a bunch of folk who were **slightly bonkers**, or to put it more politely, 'ECCENTRIC'. Someone who is eccentric is said to have an unusual or odd personality. In other words, they think and behave in ways that other people don't consider normal. But if you think that you're eccentric, you're probably not. Most eccentric people don't realize they are, whereas people who think they're eccentric or try to behave in a **'WACKY'** manner are usually just plain boring.

●

So being an eccentric, and not in the least bit BORING, Charles Babbage is an ideal first guest for our miscellany of brilliant but **BONKERS** folk.

BRILLIANT BUT BONKERS: CHARLES BABBAGE 1791–1871

✸ Like most successful creative people, Charles was madly interested in absolutely everything under the sun! And he would often put himself in danger to satisfy his endless curiosity. For instance, he once had himself roasted in an oven to 'see what would happen' (the hothead!). Even though he was in there for four minutes and the temperature was a searing 265°F (130°C), after making notes on his pulse and perspiration, he emerged from his hotspot saying that he hadn't experienced 'any great discomfort' (but did admit to being a bit upset when someone tried to cover him in goose fat and stick a sprig of parsley up his bottom).

✸ He also had himself lowered inside Mount Vesuvius so that he could get a closer look at the molten lava (the way you do). After working out that the time between eruptions was about ten minutes, he got really close to the lava then spent six minutes making notes, having allowed himself four minutes to be hauled back up before the next eruption took place (or his eyebrows caught fire).

✸ Charles was very sensitive to what he described as 'street nuisances', once listing 165 different sorts in 90 days. His most hated nuisance was organ grinders and he spent £170 to soundproof a room in his house to keep out the noise.

When someone asked if he really believed that listening to a hand organ could damage a man's brain, he replied, 'Certainly not, for the obvious reason that no man having a brain ever listened to street musicians.'

⭐ He got in touch with the poet, Alfred Lord Tennyson, about his poem 'The Vision of Sin'. This is what he said: 'In your otherwise beautiful poem, one verse reads, Every moment dies a man, Every moment one is born... If this were true, the population of the world would be at a standstill. In truth, the rate of birth is slightly in excess of that of death. I would suggest that the next version of your poem should read: Every moment dies a man, Every moment one and one-sixteenth is born. Strictly speaking, the actual figure is so long I cannot get it into a line, but I believe the figure one and one-sixteenth will be sufficiently accurate for poetry.' To which Tennyson replied:

Dear Mr S.A.D. Anorak,

You really did ought to get out more!
Alfred Lord Tennyson!

Now that's a bonkers-sounding name. Here are some more...

Six people with utterly BONKERS names

Pablo Diego José Francisco de Paula Juan Nepomuceno María de los Remedios Cipriano de la Santísima Trinidad Ruiz y Picasso

Full name of the mega-famous artist, who we usually refer to as 'Picasso' (thank goodness).

Praise-God Barebone

An English leather-seller who died in 1679. He was also a preacher (but who'd have guessed it?).

Isambard Kingdom Brunel

British engineer (1806–1859). Designed steamships, railways, bridges, tunnels and heaps more really 'big' things.

Thursday October Christian

Son of Fletcher Christian, the leader of the famous mutiny on the Bounty. Thursday was born on Thursday 14 October 1790 (well, there's a coincidence!) and died on 21 April 1831, which just happened to be … a Thursday (how obligingly tidy of him!).

Richard Plantagenet Campbell Temple-Nugent-Brydges-Chandos-Grenville

British politician and close friend of Prime Minister Benjamin Disraeli (died in 1889).

Sir Sitwell Sitwell (1769–1811)

British politician and landowner (and not a dog trainer), who just happens to be the dad of our next bonkers guest-star….

Sir George Rearsby Sitwell was EXTREMELY ECCENTRIC (not surprising really, his dad having a name like that).

Here's a list of some of the rather 'odd' things he got up to. Can you spot the ones which might have been made up?

1 Guests arriving at Sir George's huge, Derbyshire stately home, Renishaw Hall, were met with a sign which said:

I MUST ASK ANYONE ENTERING THE HOUSE NEVER TO CONTRADICT ME IN ANY WAY, AS IT INTERFERES WITH THE FUNCTIONING OF THE GASTRIC JUICES AND PREVENTS MY SLEEPING AT NIGHT

2 Sir George had all the cows on his country estate stencilled with an attractive blue-and-white Chinese Willow Pattern design because he thought it would make them 'look nicer'.

3 Whilst travelling on a train when he was a nipper, little George proudly announced to the other passengers,

'I am **Sir George Sitwell**, baronet. I am four years old and the YOUNGEST baronet in England.'

4 He had three children whom he named Osbert, Sachaverell and Edith.

5 He tried to pay his Osbert's Eton school fees in pigs and potatoes.

6 Whilst passing on handy dating tips to his sons, he once said,

'There's nothing a man likes better than a girl who's good at the PARALLEL BARS'

(and who can argue with that?).

7 The wasps that buzzed around his beloved garden drove Sir George nuts so he solved the problem by inventing a really tiny gun for shooting them. He also invented a musical toothbrush which played the tune, 'Annie Laurie'.

8 During the First World War he collected peach stones which he posted to the government, saying that they could be turned into gas masks.

9 He predicted that one day all knife handles would be made from condensed milk.

10 Despite the fact that everyone else was going mad for the newfangled, incredibly useful, absolutely brilliant new invention, home electricity, Sir George said he wanted nothing to do with it and banned it from Renishaw Hall.

11 Yes, Sir George had problems getting to grips with the modern age. A friend who was intending to telephone him, said, 'I'll give you a ring on Thursday!' When the 'ring' didn't arrive, Sir George said to his son, Osbert, 'Such a pity to promise people things and then forget about them. It is not considerate – really inexcusable.' The daft bat had been expecting his friend to give him a piece of jewellery!

12 Seven of the gigantic sitting rooms at Renishaw Hall were piled high with research notes for the books which Sir George was writing. Among the titles he was working on was the utterly enthralling 'Lepers' Squints', the unputdownable 'Acorns as an Article of Medieval Diet' and that classic page-turner, 'The History of the Fork.' Quite unsurprisingly, none of these were ever published.

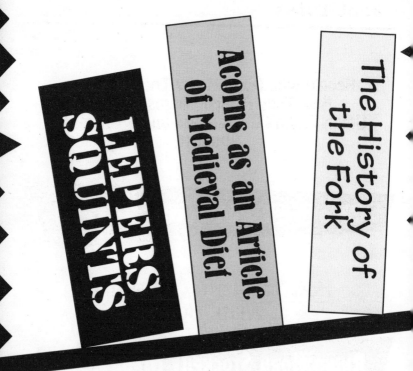

LEPERS SQUINTS

Acorns as an Article of Medieval Diet

The History of the Fork

ALL TRUE!

It wasn't just Sir George who wrote batty books. Other people do it, too. And here to prove it are...

Ten ridiculous – but totally true – book titles

People Who Don't Know They're Dead: How They Attach Themselves to Unsuspecting Bystanders and What to Do About It

Cheese Problems Solved

How To Write A How-To-Write Book

Rhino Horn Stockpile Management

Ancient Starch Research

SOIL NAILING:
BEST PRACTICE GUIDANCE

Nessus, Snort and Ethereal Powertools

Dining Posture in Ancient Rome

GREEK RURAL POSTMEN AND THEIR CANCELLATION NUMBERS

Bombproof Your Horse

And talking of horses, it's now time to meet...

'A NEIGH-LIST' CELEBRITY

During the late fifteenth and early sixteenth centuries Marocco the horse was the most famous animal in Europe. He may have been a dumb beast but he was also a talented superstar with X-factor by the cart-load!

He could count, dance, walk on two legs, both backwards and forwards, and, on command, he would not only sneeze and neigh, but would also produce an enormous bucketful of wee. Everyone who saw him was astonished by his remarkable abilities and he quickly became a top celeb of his day, with William Shakespeare referring to him in one of his plays and Sir Walter Raleigh name-checking him in a book. Marocco's owner and trainer was a man called William Banks who made lots of money by taking him on tour around Europe where, instead of pulling gigs, as most horses did in those days, Marocco performed them. Here are just a few of his many astounding tricks...

1 When William threw a glove in the air, Marocco would catch it in his teeth then take it to whichever member of the audience his master described to him. For instance if he said, 'the gentleman in the spectacles', he would carry it to the man in glasses. Or, if he said 'the lady in the purple dress', he would take it to her.

2 William would collect coins from the audience then shake them up in a large purse. Not only would Marocco pick out and return each coin to its rightful owner but he would also inform them how many pence it was worth by tapping out the coin's value with his hoof.

3 If William mentioned the Queen of England, Marocco bowed respectfully. But if he mentioned the King of Spain, this passionately patriotic pony would flatly refuse to show his respect. Then, if William persisted in trying to get Marocco to bow to the King of Spain he would go completely bananas, neighing furiously, showing his teeth and kicking out his back legs.

4 Sometimes Mr Banks would threaten to sell Marocco to a carter. Whenever he did, his crafty wonder horse would immediately fall to the floor and pretend to be dead (because, as everyone knows ... 'there's no point in flogging a dead horse').

5 After being away from London for some time, William and Marocco returned to discover that the performing animal business was really booming and the capital was now positively awash with boogying baboons, body-popping bears, disco-dancing donkeys and cavorting camels! It was time for Marocco to reassert himself as London's premier prancing pony. After climbing all 1,000 of the rickety steps of the spiral staircase which led to the flat rooftop of old St Paul's Cathedral, Marocco gave the performance of a lifetime. There, 520 feet above the ground, the super-steed strutted his stuff, shimmying, skipping and swaying to the delight of the masses of onlookers who thronged the streets below. However, one miserable old codger wasn't impressed. When summoned to his window to see the show, he asked why he should look up at a dancing horse when he could much more easily look down on the asses in the streets below (there's always one, isn't there?).

6 When Marocco did his routine in front of the less 'sophisticated' inhabitants of country places like Shrewsbury, rather than entertaining them, his antics actually scared them smockless. Many of them were said to have sat pale and trembling before the jitterbugging horse, convinced that Mr Banks was an evil sorcerer and that Marocco was not a horse at all, but a horse-shaped and extremely scary demon! (Or two really dodgy blokes hidden inside a pantomime horse costume.)

Here are **seven** more famous HORSES and their riders, but **unfortunately** there was a mix-up in the stables and they've mounted the WRONG ONES. Can you reunite them with their **owners**? ⟹

ANSWERS: 1) Duke of Wellington, Copenhagen 2) Gandalf, Shadowfax 3) Napoleon, Marengo 4) Dick Turpin, Black Bess 5) Zorro, Tornado 6) Lone Ranger, Silver 7) Roy Rogers, Trigger

Sir Astley Cooper's Waterloo Horses

After the Battle of Waterloo in 1815 all the wounded horses of the Household Brigade of Cavalry were sold off at an auction. Sir Astley Cooper, a brilliant surgeon and lover of horses, bought 12 of the most seriously injured ones and took them back to his park in the country. Then, with the help of his servants, he set about operating on the suffering animals, carefully and gently extracting bullets, shrapnel and grape-shot from their horribly mangled flesh. With lots of tender, loving care, all of the horses eventually recovered from their operations and were then let loose in the grounds of his country estate. One morning, to his great amusement and amazement, Sir Astley was astonished to see the 12 horses line up, military style, then 'cavalry charge' across the park, just as if they were back on the battlefield. After which, they retreated, formed up again and performed yet another cavalry charge, a habit which they repeated almost every day for the rest of their lives.

One day, the famous Second World War hero, General Montgomery got into a London taxi and asked the driver to take him to Waterloo.

'Station?' said the driver.

'Certainly!' replied General Montgomery. 'We're a bit late for the battle!'

Napoleon, the French emperor who was defeated at the Battle of Waterloo, also attempted to invade Russia in 1812. But that all went horribly wrong and he and his army were forced to retreat. As they fled the Russians, Napoleon received yet more bad news. There was trouble back in France as well! Terrified that someone might try and take over from him in his absence, the Emperor decided to rush home, leaving most of his army behind in Russia. Arriving at a river crossing, he asked the ferryman if he'd transported any deserters from the French army across the river yet.

'No', replied the ferryman. 'You're the first!'

NAPOLEON was a DICTATOR. In other words, a ruler who assumes total power over their people and controls them with a rod of iron. However, as well as being a TYRANT, Napoleon is generally thought to have brought some benefits to France such as an efficient road system and beautifully redesigned cities, such as Paris. **Unfortunately**, the same can't really be said of our next BONKERS guest who, like Napoleon, was a tyrant.

SAPARMURAT NIYAZOV (1940-2006)

The dottiest dictator ever? You decide!

Shy, retiring wallflower, Saparmurat Niyazov, was President of the central Asian country of Turkmenistan from 1990 to 2006. Saparmurat also called himself Turkmenbashi, which means Leader of All Turkmen (rather than He Who Bashes Turkmen). Turkmenbashi was the sort of person who is unable to walk past a mirror without pausing to admire themselves, swooning at their own magnificence and perfection. So desperate was he to share his fantabulousness with his 5 million 'subjects' that, not only did he name hundreds of streets, Turkmenbashi, but he also filled those same streets with huge gold statues of himself and thousands of posters depicting his fabulous face. He also passed a law saying that his gorgeous mug should appear on all sorts of stuff including clocks and watches, TV screens, money and bottles of booze (but, strangely enough, not toilet rolls). When a foreign journalist asked President Turkmenbashi about his need to see his face absolutely everywhere, the bashful shrinking violet modestly replied, 'If I was a worker and my president gave me all the things they have here in Turkmenistan, I would not only paint his picture, I would have his picture on my shoulder, or on my clothing. I'm personally against seeing my pictures and statues in the streets – but it's what the people want!'

Yes, he spoiled them, he really did!

Here are some other things **TURKMENBASHI** may or may not have done during his time in charge of Turkmenistan. See if you can work out which are **TRUE** and which are false.

1 He banned everyone in his country from having gold teeth and told them that the only proper way to look after their teeth was to chew bones.

2 He banned opera, circus, ballet, listening to car radios and playing CDs in public and on TV.

3 Perhaps because he was worried about what people would do with their spare time now that they couldn't visit the circus, Turkmenbashi wrote a book of his poems and his thoughts on almost every subject under the sun. He then declared that all school children must spend one day a week reading his great work. And if they hadn't learned it off by heart by the time they left school they wouldn't get a driving license, a job, or (even more worryingly), be allowed into Heaven!

4 He not only renamed the month of January, Turkmenbashi, after himself, but also the country's main airport, an entire city and a huge meteorite that landed in Turkmenistan in 1998. He also had the Turkmenistan word for bread, 'chorek', changed to his mum's name: Gurbansoltan edzhe.

5 In 2004 Turkmenbashi went on TV, announcing that he had ordered a great palace to be built, big enough to hold 1,000 people. And what had his 'brilliantness' decreed that this architectural wonder was to be made from? Ice! Yes, that stuff which quickly turns to water, especially if it happens to be in the middle of a desert. Which is precisely the place the potty president had chosen for it to be built. The loopy leader then went on to rave about how all those incredibly lucky Turkmenistan children would be able to visit the amazing ice palace and learn to ski and skate (assuming that they hadn't already drowned in the melting ice-water). And, as we all know, it's absolutely essential to know how to ski and skate when you live in a subtropical country like Turkmenistan with its long hot summers, warm dry winters and almost complete absence of snow.

6 **When he stopped smoking in 1997 Turkmenbashi passed a law banning smoking in all public places (so he wasn't a complete idiot).**

Answers: ALL TRUE!

After READING that lot you could be forgiven for thinking that Turkmenbashi was playing a **HUGE PRACTICAL JOKE** on his people. But he wasn't. They're all true! But this next story really is about a huge and ABSOLUTELY...

BONKERS, BUT BRILLIANT, PRANK!

It was November 1809 and the 22-year-old playwright, Theodore Hook, and his pal, Samuel Beazley, were walking down Berners Street in London. Just as they were passing number 54, which looked more or less like every other house in the street, not to mention tens of thousands more throughout the capital, Theodore said to Sam,

'I bet you one guinea I can make this extremely boring-looking house on this extremely boring-looking street into the most famous dwelling-place in all London, just one week from today!'

'All right!' said Samuel. 'You're on!'

Warning:

Don't even think of it! You'll get caught. You must bear in mind that this huge hoax took place at a time when there were no telephones, fax machines, or Internet. If you wanted to order a chimney sweep or a ton of coal, the only way to do it that didn't actually involve visiting the supplier, was by writing them a letter.

BTW: A guinea was a gold coin worth one pound and one shilling, or £1.05, as we'd say now. It was named after the African country of Guinea where much of the gold used to make British coins was mined in the 'Gold Coast' region. And in those days a guinea could buy you an awful lot of coal, or cakes ... or cabbages!

Our next **BONKERS** guest also enjoyed the odd PRACTICAL JOKE or two. So here's...

Some 'light' reading about Thomas Edison (1837–1931)

...as Edison's teacher decided that he was a bit of a
...it and described him as being 'addled'.

YOU'RE ADDLED BOY! YOU'LL NEVER AMOUNT TO ANYTHING!

WHAT A BRILLIANT IDEA!

So, what did Thomas do? He went on to dream up over a
thousand inventions, many of which shaped the world we live...

in today. Among his life-changing inventions were the first-ever movie camera, the first record player, first commercial, glowing light bulb and the first talking doll. His 'addled' brain was positively abuzz with activity, and when he died he left behind no less than 3,500 notebooks all brimming with ideas and sketches for new gadgets and gizmos. He also realized that we human beings never stop learning. Here are a few scintillating stories about the man who once said, 'We don't know a millionth of one percent about anything.'

✳Thomas was once asked to sign a visitor's book. When he got to the section marked 'Interests', he wrote, 'Everything'.

✳Thomas's holiday house was equipped with all sorts of labour-saving gadgets. However, an old-fashioned turnstile, so heavy that it took a real effort to get it to actually turn, blocked the path leading to the house. When someone asked him why he should have such a labour-intensive and difficult device when all around him were gadgets and gismos designed to make life so much easier, he replied, 'Well, you see, everyone who pushes that turnstile around pumps eight gallons of water into the tank on my house roof.'

✸Thomas was desperate to get the councillors of New York to give him permission to tear up the city's streets. Not because he was a vandal, but because he wanted to lay the underground cables for his dazzling new invention and light up the entire city with electricity. He invited the whole city council out to his headquarters at Menlo Park just as it was getting dark. Then he made sure that they all had to climb a very narrow staircase in the dark. They were soon stumbling and knocking into things and generally having a difficult time. By the time they finally fumbled their way to the top of the stairs, still in darkness, they were all feeling extremely bad-tempered. But then, with perfect timing, Thomas clapped his hands and the councillors instantly found themselves bathed in bright electric light. Blinking in its brilliant intensity, they looked around in wonder and saw that they were now in a large and luxurious dining hall. And before them lay a fabulous banquet prepared by New York's top chef. Naturally, Thomas was quickly told to go ahead and get ripping up the streets immediately!

✸Thomas proposed to his wife in Morse code. However, the inventor of a staggering 1093 patents had only been married to her for four weeks when he complained in his notebook,

My wife Dearly Beloved cannot invent worth a damn!

✸Thomas's friend, Henry Ford, believed that when you die, your soul leaves your body inside your very last breath. So, as Thomas lay on his deathbed Henry persuaded the great man's son, Charles Edison, to sit by his bed, test tube in hand. Then as the great genius breathed his last Charles clamped the test tube over his dad's lips, caught the breath, stoppered it with a cork and gave it to Henry. If you want to see it, the test tube with the breath in it is now in the Henry Ford Museum, Dearborn, USA.

✸Thomas nicknamed his children Dot and Dash after the symbols used in Morse code.

WELL, at least they were only **nicknames**. Dot and Dash's real names were Marion and Thomas. But you do have to feel sorry for these Victorian CHILDREN who really did get **lumbered** with these...

TEN TOTALLY BONKERS FIRST NAMES

All used between 1838 and 1900

Abisha

Babberley

Strongitharm

Tram

Murder

Brained

Lettuce

Bugless

Dozer

Despair

A POPULAR NAME from days gone by was Reginald – or Reggie for short. And this is the very SAD story of the TRAGIC END of a rag LION called Reggie.

HOW REGGIE THE RAG LION GOT MARMALISED BY THE LORD MAYOR'S ELEPHANTS

During a Lord Mayor's Show in London in the late 1920s a group of students were standing on the Thames Embankment watching the parade, accompanied by their 'pet', a life-sized, rag lion called Reggie. As each attraction passed them, the students, being students, and therefore rather over-excitable, would lift Reggie-the-rag-lion high into the air and waggle him about, cheering wildly as they did so. Then the elephants of the 'Indian Pageant' bit of the parade came plodding into view. And the students waved Reggie even more frantically and cheered even more lustily. This wasn't a good idea. The elephants didn't appreciate the lion-waggling and raucous cheering one bit. The moment they spotted Reggie leaping around and 'roaring' ferociously, they instantly assumed that they were about to be set upon by a real-life carnivore. So they did what all right-thinking elephants would do in these circumstances. They got their retaliation in first!

Roaring and trumpeting with rage, the normally gentle and well-behaved beasts tore themselves away from their keepers and charged into the crowd, ears flapping, trunks snaking and tusks scything as they bore down on their 'mane' objective: Reggie. Of course, the crowd did exactly what any right-thinking crowd would do in these circumstances and ran away! As did the students, leaving Reggie-the-rag-lion to the wrath of the enraged elephants. So, as fleeing onlookers yelled in terror and petrified police horses threw their coppers from their saddles, the furious elephants set about tearing poor Reggie to pieces. Then, having given him a jumbo-size seeing-to, the victorious tusk-force obediently returned to their positions in the parade. After a short interlude during which battered hats (and children) were knocked back into shape, wounds bandaged, bruised policemen patched up and sobbing students comforted, the procession continued on its merry way.

According to the newspapers of the day, only 30 or so people were hurt in the chaos, none of them seriously.

DID YOU KNOW?

Why are the lorries used in modern day carnival processions and pageants called floats? Well, during the early days of the Lord Mayor of London's Show, the parade took place on the River Thames itself, the attractions being mounted on boats that 'floated' past the onlookers.

Elephants are very clever. Young domestic ones in India have large bells hung around their necks so that people know where they are at all times and can therefore prevent them from getting up to mischief. But the crafty elephants have learned to scoop up a dollop of mud with their trunk and jam it in the bell to stop their clapper clanging. This means that they can raid banana plantations at night without fear of being detected.

Other Indian elephants are ridden in the rather bonkers game of elephant polo in which their riders attempt to knock a ball into a goal using long wooden mallets. Here are some more bonkers games you may not have come across...

FIVE GOOFY GAMES AND POTTY PASTIMES

1 Cow pat bingo: A field is divided into squares, each of which is given a number. Everyone 'buys' a number then a cow is let into the field and they all wait with baited breath as it wanders around chewing the cud.

Everyone watching knows that sooner or later the cow will have to deposit a 'country pancake' in one of the squares. And if it's the square they've chosen they get to win all the money.

2 The Henley-on-Todd Regatta: The very posh original version of this event, the 'Henley Regatta' boating festival is attended by people in striped blazers and straw boater hats who watch rowing crews race up and down the river. The Australian version of the regatta is held on the Todd River near Alice Springs, Australia. But there isn't any water in the Todd River so the rowers' legs stick out of the bottom of their boats and they run up and down the dry river bed, which all looks very silly!

3 Mobile phone throwing: This sport began in Finland where they manufacture lots of mobile phones and no doubt have plenty to spare. You simply throw your mobile phone as far as you can, as stylishly as you can, then you're judged on your distance and technique.

4 Bull running: This takes place in Pamplona in Spain where enormous, angry bulls charge around the town streets doing their best to kill the completely bonkers young men who deliberately put themselves in their path. As the bulls rush at them, the lads leap this way and that in order to avoid them. Often not quite quickly enough. Consequently, several young dare-devils are seriously injured or killed every year.

5 Sheep running. This is the softy's version of the bull-running in which the sheep often have little cuddly-toy jockeys strapped to their backs. Usually no one gets hurt. However, at one such event in New Zealand, a woman was knocked unconscious by the sheep (after being 'badly bleaten').

Any of them take your **fancy**?
Perhaps the BULL
RUNNING is a bit
too **tame** for you?
In that case why
not have a GO at...

Something BONKERS to do on a boring Sunday afternoon

Bull riding

How to sit on a ton of terror and live to tell the tale

FIRST A WARNING. Bull riding is very, very dangerous. Your bull will be at least twenty times bigger than you are. Or, to put it another way, you will be sitting on a ton of solid muscle. A ton of solid muscle that is extremely mean and mischievous. Your bull's main aim during the time you're on (and off) it, is to kill you. In order to do this, it will jump high into the air, spin like a dervish, kick out its back legs, twist and turn, stomp you with its hooves, gore you with its horns and try to roll over on top of you and crush you. Bet you can't wait!

Here's what to do...

1 Get fit; watch loads of bull-riding videos, then make out your will.

✦

2 Get your bull-riding outfit. This will include a vest made from body armour, a bull-riding glove, some sticky 'rosin' to rub on your glove, plus a pair of chaps. NB: They're the leather leg-covering sort of 'chaps', not the chaps who will be picking up your various body parts after you've been ripped to shreds by your bull.

✦

3 Practice bull riding on a mechanical bull. At least you can switch it off when the going gets rough.

✦

4 Enter a bull-riding contest. Say a last goodbye to your friends and family.

✦

5 Your big moment has finally arrived. First go to the chute. This is the very strong pen that will contain your bull while you mount it, severely restricting its movement and thereby saving you from injury. By the way, you can't actually choose the bull you're going to ride, for instance the really tiny, three-legged one with the glass eye and the fuzzy-felt horns. You get what you're given. But at least you won't get Bodacious, the most vicious bull-riding bull ever, so dangerous that he was eventually banned from taking part the sport.

6 Climb onto your bull's back while it's in the chute. Grasp the rope wrapped around its middle. Rub your rosin-covered glove up and down it to get the rope good and sticky. This will give you a better grip. Prepare to shoot out of the chute!

7 Now, all you have to do is stay on your bull's back for a mere eight seconds. This would be reasonably easy if you were both going to stay in the chute. But you aren't. So, say a little prayer and lock your legs around your bull. Then, when you feel as ready as you'll ever be, give a nod to the gatemen who will release your bull.

8 At this point your massive mount will go absolutely ... 'bullistic!', positively exploding into the arena! As it kicks out its back legs you'll be thrown high into the air, coming back down again with a terrible bump. Welcome to the 'House of Pain', as bull riders call it.

9 Now, if you're still on board, your bull may attempt to throw you forwards so that your face smashes into its skull and horns. This trick often breaks every bone in a bull rider's face. It will also use its back legs to kick you where the sun doesn't shine.

Useful tip:

If you're wearing your watch, resist the temptation to look at it. Each second will feel like an hour!

10 Your bull will now be going berserk and you will be tempted to use your free hand to get a better grip on it. Don't! If you do this you will be disqualified. Keep your free hand high over your head and don't let it touch any part of the bull or yourself!

11 As your bull does its best to buck you off, you must 'roll with the punches'. Bull riders don't 'fight' their bull. They 'dance' with it, trying to anticipate its every movement, matching them with their own body movements so that they stay in rhythm with the bull.

TIP: Watch the movement of your bull's head to see which way he'll go next. His body will always follow in the same direction.

12 Your bull may now start to spin so that he can throw you off by 'centrifugal' force. Try and position yourself in the middle of your bull's back and lean to the 'inside' of the spin.

13 If you're still on, it's probably time to get off your bull. This isn't easy. Whatever you do, don't try to get off your bull when he's spinning! If you do, you'll fall 'inside' the spin and he'll 'stomp' you. What you must do is lift your chin up, wait for your bull to kick, then release your hand and roll to his outside so that you fall off. If your bull's kicking he'll be moving away from you now and you'll be able to jump to your feet and run for your life. But only if you're quick enough!

You may have now realized that bull riding involves a lot of pain and injury. When asked what he thought of the sport, one young bull rider said, 'I've got metal plates around my one eye, I've had a hundred stitches in my face and shoulder separations and concussions, ripped my right bicep off my right arm and fractured all the bones in my feet, but it's worth it to go after your dream.'

DOH! Maybe it would be safer to stick to SIMPLY READING about bull riding in a **bull-riding** magazine like the one mentioned in THESE...

74

BONKERS – BUT TOTALLY TRUE – MAGAZINE TITLES

PRO BULLRIDER

Nails and Feet Magazine

POTATO REVIEW

AUSTRALIAN GOAT WORLD

Biscuit and Cracker Baker

Miniature Donkey Talk

GLOBAL SLAG MAGAZINE

DOORKNOB Collector

Now, here's another bull rider. But this one had no trouble at all staying on his bull. He even went FOX HUNTING on him. Now that sounds a bit ... **bonkers!**

JEMMY HIRST — ANIMAL CRACKERS!

Jemmy Hirst (1730–1802) was a farmer and part-time inventor from Rawcliffe in Yorkshire who was absolutely bonkers about his furred and feathered friends.

✴ When he was a boy, Jemmy had a talking jackdaw that he taught to say rude things about his teachers. He also had a pet hedgehog that would follow him to school every day. Jemmy was eventually sent to boarding school to study to be a priest, but he was soon expelled for **training the headmaster's pigs to jump hurdles** (beats cheating in spelling tests).

✴ After settling down to become a farmer, Jemmy became so wealthy and successful that he was able to spend lots of quality time with his nearest and dearest, i.e. his pets. These included a fox and an otter who were his constant companions and an enormous bull called Jupiter. Jemmy rode Jupiter like a horse, trotting him around the local villages and regularly going fox hunting on him. Jupiter really took to the fox hunting but the litter of piglets that Jemmy tried to train as foxhounds weren't nearly so adaptable and most unsportingly refused to get into the spirit of the thing (having become disgruntled by the whole stupid idea).

★ Jemmy also got Jupiter to pull his extremely weird lampshade-shaped, wickerwork carriage, complete with its en-suite wine cellar and double bed. He would pull it to the local horse races where Jemmy (something of a local fashion icon) would appear dressed in a gigantic lambskin hat and chicken-feather waistcoat. Being a bull and not a horse, Jupiter, quite understandably, found the carriage pulling a bit beyond his skill base, so Jemmy eventually replaced him with a mast and sails. His carriage trips immediately became a total breeze. However, while visiting his local town of Pontefract on a particularly windy day, he lost control of his craft and crashed through a shop window, earning himself a ban from the town.

★ As well as being wealthy, Jemmy was extremely generous and would summon the local poor and widow women to his house by blowing his hunting horn so that he could serve them tea and cakes from his favourite coffin. (It's not known if he was actually inside the coffin when he served the tea and cakes or whether he just used it as a handy picnic table.)

King George III eventually heard of Jemmy and invited to him to the palace, but Jemmy refused, saying that he was busy, 'teaching an otter to fish' (a perfectly good excuse, if ever there was one). However, possibly because the otter constantly refused to hand over its catch, he did eventually accept the invitation, turning up at the King's palace dressed in patchwork britches, red-and-white striped stockings, bright yellow boots and … an otter-skin coat! (Oh no, surely not!) His unusual appearance caused a sensation amongst the assembled toffs, so much so that one of them, the Duke of Devonshire, fell to the floor, overcome by a fit of the giggles. Believing the Duke to be in the grip of some sort of life-threatening seizure, Jemmy immediately leapt at him, pinching his Grace's nose tight shut and throwing a glass of water in his face because, as he put it later, 'the poor man were 'avin' 'sterics'.

In his will Jemmy said that his coffin should be carried by 12 virgin maidens and accompanied by a bagpiper and fiddler playing happy music but the village of Rawcliffe could only manage two virgin maidens so the widow women had to do the carrying instead. Jemmy now has a pub named after him in the rather cheekily named town of Goole.

Beware the KILLER pouffe!

If you go bull riding and fox hunting you're asking for bruises, broken bones and worse. But if you stay in that safe and cosy place known as home, you'll be well out of harm's reach, won't you? Well, unless you're very careful, you won't! Your house is bristling with all manner of terrifying booby traps just lying around waiting for you to make a wrong move. When you do, they pounce, breaking your bones, blocking your airways, searing your flesh and slashing your skin. And what makes it worse, is that they're disguised as innocent everyday objects such as trousers, tea-cosies, and false teeth! It's not just clumsy-clots who this stuff happens to. After all, if ex-Wimbledon goalkeeper, David Beasant, can drop a bottle of salad cream on his foot and nearly slice off his big toe, it can happen to anyone. Read on ... and be terrified!

Your house is bristling
with all manner of
TERRIFYING booby traps

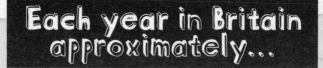

Each year in Britain approximately...

700 children get marbles stuck up their noses.

16,000 people are injured by the cushions known as pouffes.

2,000 people are injured trying to open tins of corned beef.

1,500 people have hospital treatment for accidents involving tissue paper.

37,000 people are treated for accidents involving slippers.

50 people are injured by Blu-Tack.
100 people end up in hospital because of cricket stumps.

67,000 people are injured trying to peel the cellophane off a packet of sandwiches, open a ready-meal or open a ring-pull can.

11,500 people are taken to hospital because of accidents with socks, tights or stockings.

And the list goes on ... shoes: 370,000 injuries; hair brushes: 390; vegetables: 14,000; piles of ironing: 5,200; cotton-wool buds: 8,569; false teeth: 933; clothes baskets: 2768; toilet roll holders: 287; brillo pads: 226; talcum powder: 123; deodorants: 431; beanbags: 738; airing cupboards: 246.

Oh yes! And 5,000 people are injured by their own trousers every year.

NOW, there could well be a **special word** for being injured by your own trousers. Find out if there is BY DOING THIS...

COMPLETELY BONKERS WORDS QUIZ

1 STRIDEWALLOP

a) an injury caused whilst putting on your trousers
b) a very painful type of rugby tackle
c) a tall and awkward woman

2 SLUBBERDEGULLION

a) a large sailing ship, in need of repair
b) a filthy slob
c) a seagull-eating glutton

3 SNIRTLE

a) a short suppressed snigger
b) a flowery silk neck tie
c) to blow your nose on your sleeve

4 SHANGLE

a) a layer of sharp stones, usually found on a beach
b) to fasten a tin or kettle to a dog's tail
c) to walk up to someone sideways

5 UBERTY

a) the process of changing from a child to a grown up
b) a lot of something
c) a word describing someone who's posh and stuck-up as in, ''E's a bit 'uberty!'

6 OXYMORON

a) a stupid person fond of large cattle
b) a person addicted to crosswords
c) putting together two words with opposite meanings

7 SNOLLYGOSTER

a) an incredibly strong wind that blows birds inside out
b) a monster which eats children and chickens
c) a ghost only seen when it's snowing

8 SNOOL

a) a really creepy person
b) very runny snot
c) someone who thinks they're good at snooker but is actually rubbish

9 POZZY WALLAH

a) someone who loves jam
b) a Medieval servant whose job it was to empty toilets
c) someone who always looks on the bright side

10 PALINDROME

a) a large, hemisphere-shaped place where you meet your friends
b) the opposite of a sun-tanning booth
c) a word, phrase or number which can be read the same in either direction

Answers: 1c 2a 3b 4b 5c 6b 7a 8a 9c 10c

And just to prove
that the last answer
is the **CORRECT** one,
here are...

TEN PALINDROMES FOR YOU TO TRY

Lisa Bonet ate no basil

Go deliver a dare, vile dog!

Kay, a red nude, peeped under a yak

Don't nod

Madam, in Eden I'm Adam

God saw I was dog

Never odd or even

May a moody baby doom a yam?

Go hang a salami; I'm a lasagna hog!

A Toyota! Race fast ... safe car: a Toyota

Our next **BONKERS** hero didn't go bull riding but she was DESPERATE to EXPERIENCE some truly dangerous situations. And when she did finally get her WISH, she handled the hazards in a way that would have made **Indiana Jones** green with envy.

MARY, MARY, DOES NOTHING SCARE THEE?

Mary Kingsley spent the first 30 years of her life looking after her sick mother and father. She didn't go to school and never travelled further than the family home. But then her mum and dad died and she decided that she'd like to explore the **crocodile-infested jungles** of Africa.

Other people told her she'd be bonkers to go there. One woman said that she knew of a man who had come back from Africa 'an aged wreck of forty' with jungle fever so bad that he shook so much 'as to dislodge a chandelier, thereby destroying a valuable tea-service and flattening the silver teapot in its midst!'. Someone else told her she should wear men's clothes to protect her from scorpions, snakes, mosquitoes and the thousand other dangers that lay in wait for her.

So Mary put on her Victorian lady's enormous woollen skirt, petticoats, corset, tight-waisted, high-collared blouse and small fur cap and set off. All she took with her was a few hundred pounds, a bag, some collecting boxes, her umbrella and a book of phrases of the sort guaranteed to make you really popular with the locals, such as, 'Get up, you lazy scamps!' and 'Why has not this man been buried?', plus the genuinely useful, 'Help, I am drowning!'

She first visited crocodile-infested mangrove swamps in order to search for rare plants, insects and fish. And it wasn't long before a crocodile tried to climb into her canoe.

However, Mary wasn't fazed one bit, recalling that this 'pushing young creature who had not learnt manners ... chose to get his front paws over the stern of my canoe' and that she was forced to 'fetch him a clip on the snout with a paddle!'

Next, Mary stayed with the cannibal tribe known as the Fang. Whilst sleeping in one of their huts Mary smelled a horrid pong. On investigating a bag hanging on the hut wall she found that it contained a human hand, three big toes, two ears and four eyes (just a light snack then).

Once, Mary fell into an animal trap. If she'd been wearing men's clothes, she would have died most horribly. But her thick Victorian skirts and petticoats protected her from the stakes that were poking up from the bottom of the pit. Her African guides rushed to the edge of the hole and asked Mary, 'You kill?', to which she calmly replied, 'Not much.'

Later, Mary found a hippopotamus had parked itself between her and her canoe. 'I wanted one of us to leave,' she recalled. 'I preferred it should be myself.' Then, ignoring the fact that hippos kill more people in Africa than any other animal, she went up to it and scratched it behind the ear with her umbrella. 'We parted on good terms!' she said later.

Mary also had various encounters with leopards. She rescued one from a trap but when the ungrateful beast began sniffing her skirts quite menacingly, she simply said to it, 'Go home, you fool!' And it did! At another time, she came upon a leopard attacking a dog and hurled a chair at the leopard which then turned on her. But, before it could do any damage, she clobbered it on the head with a clay pot and it ran off.

Mary next went to South Africa and worked as a nurse during the Boer War, tending the bayonet, blast and bullet wounds of enemy prisoners. In true Mary style she said, 'Whether I shall come up out of this, I don't know … it is doubtful. The stench, the washing, the enemas, the bed pans, the blood, is my world. Not London society'.

Not long after this, she caught typhoid, dying at the tragically young age of 37.

One of the **DANGERS** Mary braved in Africa was MOSQUITOES, those pesky insects which have killed more people than anything else in the world. One of the diseases that mosquitoes pass on is yellow fever. One researcher went to some very EXTREME MEASURES in his investigations into yellow fever. To find out about the weird and completely disgusting things he did, read on. But only if you've got a STRONG STOMACH!

CARE FOR A SPOT MORE F'FRIED SICK, MR FFIRTH?

During the early 19th century Stubbins Ffirth (1784–1820) set out to prove that yellow fever isn't contagious. This is how he did it.

a) He made cuts in his arms then got some fresh, black bile, newly puked up by yellow fever victims and poured it into the wounds.

b) Alas, poor Stubbins didn't get the yellow fever so he next tried dribbling the vomit into his own eyes. He didn't get yellow fever (although he did have to give his specs a really good wash afterwards).

✴

c) He next began smearing the bodily crud from yellow fever victims over his own body, including all sorts of disgusting stuff like their blood, spit, sweat and wee. Once more he didn't catch the fever (but he did wonder why no one would sit next to him on the bus).

✴

d) His next brainwave was to create what can only be described as a 'puke-arium' where he heated up great dollops of steaming puke so that it filled the room with billowing clouds of foul-smelling 'vomit-vapour'. He then sat there, enthusiastically inhaling great lungfuls of sick-steam. Afterwards, apart from suffering from a really bad headache, Stubbins said he generally felt 'quite well'.

✴

e) Finally he thought to himself, 'There's nothing for it! The only way I'm going to catch yellow fever is to actually eat some sick! First he took in his vomit 'hygienically', in the form of a pill made from some good wholesome puke. But then Stubbins cried something like, 'Oh what the sickens! In for a penny in for a pound!' and got his patients to 'blow their groceries' (sophisticated medical term for being sick) directly into his own open mouth.

Needless to say, he didn't catch yellow fever.

By now, heartily 'sick to the back teeth' of his whole experiment, he came to the conclusion that it's impossible to catch yellow fever and packed in playing around with other people's puke. He was wrong! All the sick he had used had been thrown up by patients in the late stages of the disease and therefore it was no longer contagious.

The only way I'm going to catch yellow fever is to actually eat some SICK!

Now here's a TRICK
that Mary Kingsley
may well have
found useful during
her **jungle**
adventures. It's
our next...

SOMETHING BONKERS TO DO ON A BORING SUNDAY AFTERNOON

How to HYPNOTIZE an alligator

What you need: one alligator, either a full grown one or a baby one.

NB: If you're new to this or are feeling a bit nervous about the whole exercise, it's probably a good idea to start with a really small alligator.

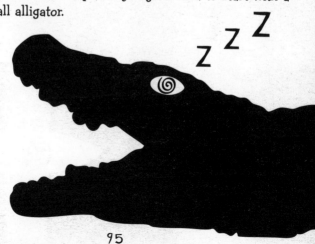

What to do:

1 Approach your alligator from the rear – you must do this quite stealthily.

2 Now carefully manoeuvre yourself into position so that you end up standing over your alligator with your feet either side of its neck.

3 Next, without any hesitation whatsoever, grasp your alligator's head with both hands, one on either side. Important safety note: whilst doing this you must make sure that you're holding the creature's jaws tight shut. If you don't do this, the alligator will eat you.

4 Now for the really tricky bit. With one smooth and confident action, raise the alligator's head then flip its entire body over so that it ends up lying on its back.

5 Quickly press your hand flat on the underside of your alligator's mouth, leaving it there for about 10 seconds.

6 If you've done everything right, your alligator will now enter a trance-like state which can last for hours. In other words the alligator is yours to do with as you please. You might like to dress it in a baby-grow, or paint it with zebra stripes.

However, if you've done it wrong the alligator will not only be wide awake, but will also be extremely annoyed with you.

How to WAKE UP your alligator

Tickle your alligator under the chin, more or less on the same spot where you pressed down your hand some time earlier.

Run away as fast as you can! You might even wish to get into shape for the 'running-away' bit by entering a marathon. But if you do, try to finish it in a reasonable time.

How time flies when you're having a run.

Top athlete completes Stockholm Marathon. His time? A mere ... 55 years!

Champion long-distance runner, Shizo Kanakuri, disappeared while running the marathon in the 1912 Summer Olympics in Stockholm. Despite huge police searches, Shizo couldn't be found so the Swedish authorities listed him as an official missing person, assuming that something awful had happened to him. However, 50 years later, in 1962, a journalist discovered Shizo living in Japan. Here's what happened...

IT WAS A PARTICULARLY SWELTERING HOT DAY. SOON SHIZO WAS GASPING FOR A DRINK.

COR! I COULD JUST DRINK ONE OF THEM!

WOULD YOU MIND IF I HAD A DRINK?

OF COURSE NOT! AND SIT DOWN FOR A MINUTE!

THE TEMPTATION WAS TOO MUCH!

Perhaps Shizo had decided to do his 'runner' after reading the first title on our next batch of...

BONKERS — BUT TOTALLY TRUE — BOOK TITLES

Better Never To Have Been: The Harm of Coming Into Existence in third place

PROCEEDINGS OF THE SECOND INTERNATIONAL WORKSHOP ON NUDE MICE

THE STRAY SHOPPING CARTS OF EASTERN NORTH AMERICA

American Bottom Archaeology

RE-USING OLD GRAVES

VERSAILLES: The View From Sweden

MONUMENTAL BEGINNINGS: ARCHAEOLOGY OF THE N4 SLIGO INNER RELIEF ROAD

The Joy of CHICKENS

And what a **joy** CHICKENS can be — especially if they're anything like the one in our next **BONKERS**, but totally true story. Then again, perhaps NOT!

MIKE THE HEADLESS CHICKEN

How to keep your head when all about are losing theirs (well, almost)

Most people know that, after they've had their heads chopped off, chickens sometimes run around for a minute or so before finally dropping dead. But what they don't normally do is continue to live days, or even weeks and months, after being decapitated, whilst also attempting to crow! However, one chicken did exactly this. Check out this interview with its owner to find out the facts.

Interviewer: So, Mr Olsen, how did this amazing story begin?

Mr Olsen: *It all started on September 10th 1945. I was killing chickens on my farm in Fruita, Colorado. Well, you know how it is! After being 'chopped', a few of them ran around for a while like ... ha ha, 'headless chickens'. But then they dropped dead.*

I: As they do!

Mr O: *Sure! Now came the turn of the cockerel we called Mike. I lopped off his head then went on to chop a few more. But now I noticed something real odd. Because, even though Mike's durn head had been lying on the ground for a good ten minutes, he was still strutting around the cotton-pickin' farmyard!*

I: Wow!

Mr O: *Yes! And that crazy critter strutted his stuff for the rest of the day! And the next! And the one after that!*

I: Astounding!

Mr O: *'Well!' I thought 'This is one amazing bird I have here. I'll feed him and see what happens next.' So, using an eyedropper, I fed ground-up grain and water into Mike's food pipe. And Mike thrived, acting just like a normal rooster!*

I: How could he do that?

Mr O: *Well, not only did he sit on his perch and try to cock-a'doodle-do—*

I: Or 'cock-a'doodle-don't'?

Mr O: *But he also busily preened himself!*

I: With the non-existent beak which had once been attached to his non-existent head!

Mr O: *Got it in one! 'Well!' I thought. 'I can make money out of this bird!'*

I: And it wouldn't be chicken feed!

Mr O: *Too true! I took Mike on a tour of the USA and made thousands of dollars from charging people to see him strut his stuff.*

I: I understand he did this alongside a jam jar containing his ex-head.

Mr O (**whispering**): *Actually, it was another chicken's head. Our cat ate Mike's not long after I chopped it off.*

I: But who was to know?

Mr O: *Exactly! Well, Mike lived for another 18 months, strutting and preening and cock-a'doodling and amazing all who set eyes on him.*

I: But then something went wrong?

Mr O: *Yup! One night, me and my wife and Mike were in a hotel room when he began choking on his own mucus! Now normally I'd remove this mucus with a syringe. But I'd forgotten the durn thing!*

I: So Mike choked to death?

Mr O (sniffling): *Yup! But we still remember him here in Fruita on our annual Mike the Headless Chicken Day. We get up to all sorts of crazy stuff, like 'Run Like a Headless Chicken Race', the 'Pin the Head on the Chicken' game and 'Chicken Poo Bingo'.*

I: Whilst eating lots and lots of … chicken?

Mr O: *Eggzactly!*

So why did Mike survive his beheading? Well, Mr Olsen didn't quite cut off all his head and one of Mike's ears escaped the axe. Also, the chop actually missed Mike's jugular vein and a blood clot stopped him from bleeding to death. A chicken's brain stem, as opposed to its brain, controls most of its reflex actions and Mike's brain stem was mainly unharmed. Mike was also examined by various animal protection people, who all decided that he hadn't suffered in any way (apart from having his head chopped off).

Mike and his pals may well have ended up as part of a serving of **'cackle and frog sticks'** or, if they hadn't got past being an egg, being dished up as 'cackle fruit on a raft'. But only if they'd been served up in one of the old-fashioned American restaurants where waiters spoke the very lively and IMAGINATIVE LANGUAGE known as **'diner lingo'**. Diner lingo was used by waiters right up until the 1970s, partly because it was fun and relieved the BOREDOM and frustration of a difficult job but also because it was often more easily recognizable in NOISY restaurants when waiters shouted their orders to the cook. Would you have made a good diner waiter or waitress? **Find out** by taking...

MATCH THE DINER SLANG TO THE TRANSLATION.

1 Nervous pudding
2 Put out the lights and cry
3 Sea dust
4 Radar range
5 Eve with a lid on
6 Life preservers
7 Paint it red
8 Two cows, make them cry
9 Pigs in a blanket
10 Bailed hay
11 Belch water
12 Mike and Ike
13 Cow paste
14 Whistleberries
15 Keep off the grass
16 Noah's boy
17 Dough well done with cow to cover
18 Chicks on a raft
19 On the hoof
20 Burn one, take it through the garden and pin a rose on it

a) Two hamburgers with onions
b) Any kind of meat cooked rare
c) Eggs on toast
d) Beefburger with lettuce, tomato and onion
e) Salt
f) Baked beans
g) Apple pie
h) Microwave
i) Butter
j) Buttered toast
k) Ham
l) No salad
m) Shredded wheat
n) Sparkling water
o) Sausage sandwich
p) Put tomato sauce on it
q) Doughnuts
r) Jelly
s) Salt and pepper
t) Liver and onions

Answers: 1r) 2t) 3e) 4h) 5j) 6q) 7p) 8a) 9o) 10m) 11n) 12s) 13i) 14f) 15l) 16k) 17j) 18c) 19b) 20d)

Oh, and by the way, cackle and frog sticks is chicken and chips!

Our next **BONKERS**
guest might well ha
enjoyed diner slang
He certainly had a
way with WORDS!

→

WILLIAM ARCHIBALD SPOONER
1844–1930

The Oxford priest and professor, William Spooner, was the sort of person who might go in his local hardware shop and ask for a pink slug, a trouse map, a flat cap and a well-boiled icicle when the things he really wanted were a sink plug, a mouse trap, a cat flap and a well-oiled bicycle. These sort of manguage lix-ups, sorry, language mix-ups in which, usually, the first sounds of two or more words are swapped are now known as Spoonerisms because the Reverend Spooner is said to have made many frequent and hilarious tips-of-the slongue. Actually, many so-called Spoonerisms are made up ones, having been originally inspired by William's mistakes. However, he is generally thought to have definitely come out with howlers like…

'Is the bean dizzy?' when he meant to ask, 'Is the dean busy?'

'You have hissed all my mystery lectures. You have tasted a whole worm. Please leave Oxford on the next town drain!' when what he meant to say was, 'You have missed all my history lectures. You have wasted a whole term. Please leave Oxford on the next down train!'

'The kinquering congs their titles take,' when he meant to say, 'The conquering kings their titles take.'

Here are some SPOONERISMS he may well not have said, but are fun anyway. See if you can work out what should have been said.

1 Mardon me, padam, this pie is occupewed. Can I sew you to another sheet?

2 He delivered his enemy a blushing crow.

3 I spied a huge fleet of cattle ships and bruisers.

4 Oh, what a nosy little cook!

5 When the Queen visits our school we'll have all the hags flung out. And we will not display any mad banners.

6 The Lord is our shoving leopard.

7 Not now, I'm busy fighting a liar.

8 The doctor stuck his hypodemic nurdle into my arm.

9 Ouch! I've just hit my bunny phone!

10 At weddings it is kisstomary to cuss the bride

Answers:
1 Pardon me, madam, this pew is occupied. Can I show you to another seat?
2 He delivered his enemy a crushing blow.
3 I spied a huge fleet of battle ships and cruisers.
4 Oh, what a cosy little nook!
5 When the Queen visits our school we'll have all the flags hung out. And we will most definitely not display any bad manners.
6 The Lord is our loving shepherd.
7 Not now, I'm busy lighting the fire.
8 The doctor stuck his hypodermic needle into my arm.
9 Owch! I've just hit my funny bone!
10 At weddings it is customary to kiss the bride.

And that last one brings us NICELY to these ...

TWELVE FASCINATING FACTS ABOUT ... KISSING!

1 When you kiss someone you exchange between 10 million and 1 billion of your bacteria.

2 When the first steam trains began operating in Britain women were advised to put pins between their lips in case strange men tried to kiss them when the trains went into tunnels.

3 During medieval times kissing people with leprosy was popular amongst high-up religious bods like priests and bishops. It was their way of saying, 'We don't consider ourselves too superior to give a big, sloppy smackeroo to that highly infectious and somewhat cruddy person.' (Even if their lips did drop off while we were doing it.)

4 Chimpanzees kiss with their mouths open but they don't stick out their tongues and waggle them about when they do it. However, their much brainier and gentler cousins, bonobos, kiss with open mouths and do the tongue waggling thing.

5 As part of their training to become completely gross and 100 per cent evil, medieval witches were said to have had to kiss the Devil's bottom.

6 And talking of kisses on the bottom: people put little 'x's at the end of letters and emails because the shape is said to represent two pairs of lips making contact (but why maths teachers feel the need to put all those kisses on their pupils' work is anyone's guess).

7 The very passionate kissing of the South Pacific Trobriand Islanders usually ends up with them biting off each other's eyelashes (then choking to death).

8 Seventy per cent of people aged between 16 and 24 had their first kiss by the time they are 15 while the other 30 per cent have had their first kiss by the time they are 5 (but that's usually from their Gran).

9 The word 'kiss' comes from the Old English word, 'cyssan' ('to snog'). Cyssan is almost certainly an onomatopeiac word. Or to put it another way, when you say it, it sounds like the noise which is made when two people kiss (or let the air out of a balloon really slowly).

10 Not everyone likes kissing. When the Tsonga people of southern Africa first saw Europeans kissing in 1927, they were genuinely disgusted, saying, 'Look at these people! They suck each other! They eat each other's saliva and dirt!'

11 An Israeli woman accidentally bit off part of her boyfriend's tongue while they were having an extra passionate snog but doctors later sewed it back on (however, when she tried to give them a 'thank-you' peck on the cheek, they all ran away).

12 The average person spends 336 hours of their life kissing.

Have you ever **wondered** about all the other stuff we do during our lifetime, such as how many words we speak, how many times we go to the LOO, how much sick we puke up – delicate but **fascinating stuff** like that! Well, wonder no more!

Reader, this ... is your life!
Your questions answered

How many more are there like me?

You're currently one of the 6.7 billion or so human beings living on planet earth. Or, to put it another way, you make up one 6,776,844,256th of the world's population. Well, you did until a few seconds ago, but while you were reading that sentence, another 300 new babies were born (or 525, if you're a slow reader).

How long will I live for?

If they're lucky, most people currently keep on breathing until they're about 78 years old. Well that's unless they happen to have been born somewhere like the African countries of Sierra Leone, Zimbabwe and Swaziland, where, with luck, they'll manage a measly 37 birthdays before they'll finally peg out. Or Afghanistan, where they might just get to enjoy 42.

How much will I eat during my entire life?

During your time in this world you'll munch your way through a positive mountain of nosh, including an astoun

4 cows, 21 sheep, 15 pigs, 1,200 chickens, 13,345 eggs, 4,283 bread loaves, 5,130 pounds of spuds, 5,272 apples, 845 cans of baked beans and 10,000 chocolate bars (or, if you're an author, 500,000 chocolate bars).

How much will I drink during my life?

You'll slurp down an entire lake's-worth of fluids including 16,000 pints of milk, 16,000 gallons of water, 10,351 pints of beer, 1,694 bottles of wine and 74,802 cups of tea.

How much body waste will I get rid of during my life?

Obviously, as you're consuming your lifetime's staggering 50 tonnes worth of nosh you'll be needing to be getting get rid of the 'not-so-useful' bits at regular intervals (or risk painfully and embarrassingly … exploding!). So on average, you'll go to the loo six times a day and one of those visits will be for the pongier stuff which, because your body is so brilliant at extracting the good from the bad and ugly, will finally come in (or should that be out?) at a mere three tonnes.

…se, in order to clean up after dumping all that you'll also get through a total of 4,239 toilet

while we're discussing revolting stuff, you'll …usting 49 litres of sick.

✳ And when you were a nipper, quite unable to control all these comings and goings, you would have got through a nose-wrinkling 3,800 disposable nappies in the first two and a half years of your messy little life and squirted out a whopping, not to mention, sopping, 254 litres of wee.

But life's not all about eating, drinking and going to the loo. So, tell me about some of the other things I'll be doing?

Well, you'll have 7,163 baths (hopefully), wash your hair 11,500 times, unless you happen to go bald, (in which case you'll just need the occasional polish), dream 104,390 dreams, read 2,455 newspapers and 533 books (or, fingers crossed, loads and loads more than that). In order to stay healthy you'll see a doctor 314 times (and loads more than that if you happen to marry one) and you'll take 30,000 tablets (but preferably not all at once).

And what about the things I'll be buying and using?

Once you've started earning and spending, you'll end up having owned no less than 3.5 washing machines, 3.4 fridges, 3.2 microwave ovens, 4.2 televisions, 9.8 DVD players, 15 computers and 8 cars! And when you've finished driving those cars you'll have travelled 728,480 km (452,656 miles) in them. That would be like driving to the moon and back. NB: You won't have actually owned 'half' a washing machine or '0.2' of a computer (unless you're very, very weird). These figures are all statistical averages.

And finally, tell me about me and all the other people I'll meet?

You'll have about 1,700 friends and acquaintances during your lifetime. Sadly, but inevitably, 99 of them will eventually die from lung cancer, 305 from heart disease, 179 from strokes and 111 from flu or pneumonia. Which still leaves about 1,000 who'll die from other things, such as old age and being eaten by grizzly bears or alligators). While you're with those friends, not to mention all the other people you meet, you'll speak between 2,000 and 4,000 words every day, if you're a boy, and between 6,400 and 8,000 words if you're a girl (but hardly any words at all if you become a Trappist monk).

I WANNA **LIVE** FOR EVER!

Most people in rich developed countries now expect to live until they're nearly 80. But many children born in the 21st century (for instance, you, young reader!) are expected to keep going until they are at least 100! And who knows, in centuries to come, with the help of artificial body parts (and lots of Long Life milk), humans may well go on for ever! Just look at the ages people got to in the past and you'll see how things have come on!

Neolithic folk lasted a pathetic 20 years, if they were lucky!

Ancient Greeks and Romans managed an average 28 birthday celebrations.

Medieval folk got to 33, but only if they tried really really hard.

At the end of 18th century, very careful people got to 37.

In the early 20th century quite a few people were lasting as long as a staggering 50 years.

And around 1940, some bods were achieving what was then thought to be a whopping great 65 years.

One of the MAIN REASONS we last so long compared to folk from **bygone times** is because of huge advances in medicine and HEALTH care. However, this progress didn't come easy. Many doctors and scientists made incredible **SACRIFICES** to bring us the treatments we all benefit from nowadays, as you'll discover from this story of two utterly BONKERS BOFFINS...

BASH ON REGARDLESS, DOCTOR!

There were once two German doctors called August. One of them, Dr August Bier (let's call him Big August), wanted to find a safer way of giving people a local anaesthetic before an operation because the old-fangled general knock-you-out-completely anaesthetic methods like using chloroform or ether were extremely dodgy: one drop too much and your patient would pop their clogs before you'd even got to work on them. Big August had the idea of injecting a smidge of cocaine into the spinal fluid which surrounds the nerves along which messages pass between brain and the rest of our body, thus completely deadening the body, but leaving the patient completely conscious. Wanting to find out how effective it was, he asked his second-in-command, Dr August Hildebrandt, (we'll call him Little August) to help him with a few experiments. What happened next turned out to be nothing less than a melodrama mixed with a comedy, a farce and a tragedy, all served up with tons of slapstick and huge helpings of utter horror! So, what better way to tell the story than as a playscript. But be warned – this is going to hurt – quite a lot actually!

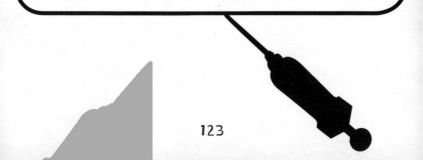

Ouch!

It's 1898. The two doctors are in their laboratory

Big August: You make ze hole in my neck zen inject a dash of cocaine into it and ve'll see how vell it works!

(Little August makes a hole in Big August's neck and prepares to inject the cocaine.)

Little August: Oh, mein gott! I've got zer wrong size injecting needle. Heng on a mo', vill you!

(But it's too late! Large amounts of precious spinal fluid are now spurting out of the hole in Big August's neck. He eventually plugs it with surgical dressing and the life-threatening leak stops.)

Little August: Sorry about zat, matey! Tell you vot! You inject me vith the cocaine!

Big August: Alvight then, tvinkletoes, I vill!

(He injects Little August. They wait for the drug to take effect. Big August gives Little August's toes a playful little tickle.)

BA: Zis little piggy went to market, zis little piggy went home. Feel anything?

LA: No, not a thing!

BA: What about zis?

(He picks up a knife and stabs Little August in the thigh. Blood fountains from the wound.)

LA: No, didn't feel a thing!

BA: All right, what about … ZIS!

(Big August stubs his burning cigar out on Little August's other leg. His flesh sizzles angrily.)

LA: No, not a sausage!

BA: (getting more carried away by the moment) All right … what about … ZIS!

(He suddenly grasps the shortest and curliest hairs on Little August's body and pulls out an entire fistful.)

LA: (grinning cheerfully) No! I 'em not feeling a thing!

(All at once, Big August grasps the hairs on little August's chest and pulls them out.)

LA: (leaping into the air): Yeeaaaaaoaeeowch! Now, ZAT veally hurt!

BA: Hmm, ziz eez veeeeery interesting...

(He strokes his moustache thoughtfully then, without warning, grasps those bits of Little August's anatomy, which, in top medical circles, are invariably referred to as 'the nadgers'. He tugs them viciously.)

LA: Aaagh! OOORAGH! OWCH! GERROFF!

(Ignoring Little August's screams of agony, Big August now, not only begins furiously belting his colleague's shin with a hammer, but also stabs his thigh again, whilst also enthusiastically squashing one of the aforementioned 'nadgers')

LA: ZE PAIN IS EXCWUCIATING! BY ZE CRINGE, STOP IT WILL YOU!

(Big August watches Little August writhing in agony.)

BA (thoughtfully): Yes, I zink ze cocaine might vell be vearing off now. How about ve go for something to eat?

LA: OORAGH! OWCH! Sounds good to me! OOOGH ... AAGH!

THE END

Afterword

The next morning (after having lost such a lot of spinal fluid) Big August woke up with a terrible headache and decided to take the day off work. But first he contacted Little August and said something like, 'Look old chap, got a bit of a headache so I'm taking a sicky. Which means you're going to have to hold the fort at the surgery, old bean. Toodle pip!'

So, the badly battered and burnt Little August had to drag himself to the surgery and treat double his normal amount of patients for the next nine days while Big August recovered from his headache.

Unsurprisingly, August and August fell out soon after this. However, despite the mishaps, the experiment was considered to be a great success, and two years later, surgeons in operating theatres all over the world were using Big August's spinal anaesthesia technique.

UNLIKE HUMANS, the amount of time animals **survive** has stayed more or less the same over the years. Match the animal to its AVERAGE LIFESPAN in our...

ANIMAL LIFETIME QUIZ

1 Cat   a) 50

2 Camel   b) 40

3 Bull   c) 6 months

4 Large dog   d) 193

5 Mouse   e) 10

6 Crocodile   f) 45

7 Worker ant   g) 25

8 Pigeon   h) 28

9 Tiger   i) 26

10 Horse   j) 4

11 Rabbit   k) 5

12 Elephant   l) 9

13 Galapagos tortoise   m) 70

14 Queen bee   n) 18

15 Blackbird   0) 22

ANSWERS:
1 g) Cat 25
2 a) Camel 50
3 h) Bull 28
4 e) Large dog 10
5 j) Mouse 4
6 f) Crocodile 45
7 c) Worker ant 6 months

8 i) Pigeon 26
9 o) Tiger 22
10 b) Horse 40
11 l) Rabbit 9
12 m) Elephant 70
13 d) Galapagos tortoise 193
14 k) Queen bee 5
15 n) Blackbird 18

OF COURSE, another reason that people in the past didn't live nearly as long as modern folk was that life was filled with all sorts of **deadly dangers**. Lives were not only cut short by accidents, DISEASES and VIOLENCE, but also by the lawmakers themselves! Make one wrong move and you might find yourself dangling from the **HANGMAN'S NOOSE!**

Good noose! Bad noose!

Ten completely bonkers things you could be hanged for

The lawmakers of the past had a 'zero tolerance' attitude to bad behaviour. In Britain in 1810 there were 222 different 'offences' you could be strung up for. Here are just 10 of them.

1 Lying in wait to disfigure someone's nose. This law had been introduced in 1671, partly to stop jealous sweethearts cutting off the conks of the ladies who'd pinched their boyfriends.

2 Stealing wigs. People posing as bakers would walk around with baskets on their shoulders. However, instead of it containing bread, a small child would be hidden inside the basket. On passing someone with a particularly fine-looking wig, the child would pop up, snatch the wig from the victim's head then duck back down again. In 1722 James Appleton was hung at Tyburn for stealing three wigs.

3 Shoplifting something worth more than five shillings. That would be about £30 in today's money.

✳

4 Being out at night with a blackened face. Which was a bit unfortunate if you happened to be coal miner working a nightshift or come from tropical Africa.

✳

5 Stealing a hat. In 1750 a man called Beckford was hung for doing just this.

6 Wearing a disguise. Fancy dress parties may well have lost their popularity when this law was introduced.

✦

7 Begging. And they meant it! In 1816 four boys, aged between 9 and 13, did the 'hempen jig', as hanging was then known, for asking passers-by for money.

✦

8 Impersonating a Chelsea Pensioner.

✦

9 Attempting suicide. So, having tried to kill yourself and failed, the authorities would finish the job for you.

✦

10 Being in the company of gypsies for more than a month. A fourteen-year-old girl was hanged for this in 1782.

Some people are better at **surviving** than others. Especially if they're as **TOUGH** and **DETERMINED** as our next die-hard (and completely **bonkers**) guest. He makes **Bruce Willis** look like Andy Pandy!

Yoo hoo, Hiroo! You can come out now, honest!

Hiroo Onoda was a fanatically loyal Japanese soldier who fought for his country, courageously doing all manner of dastardly deeds like blowing-up enemy weapons, dumps, assassinating guards and bumping off collaborators.

However, when the Second World War finally ended, Hiroo continued with his assassinating and bombing. And, quite amazingly, almost thirty years after that ... he was still at it! Find out why by reading...

Hiroo Onoda's Secret Lost Diary

1942: I have joined the Japanese army and am learning guerilla warfare. It is very exciting! Instead of doing face-to-face fighting, we do sneaky stuff such as hiding in caves and milk-churns and potting sheds then creeping up on our enemies in the dead of night and surprising them by strangling them, blowing-up their weapons store (or telling them that Santa isn't real). We have also learned loads of useful stuff like how to singlehandedly destroy an aircraft carrier using just a firework and a catapult, how to live off fried daffodils for a year and how to light a fire with just a mushroom and some mud ... that sort of thing.

December 26, 1944: I am on the Philippine jungle island of Lubang where I have joined up with some more guerillas. We have been ordered to destroy the airport and harbour (then, maybe after that, we will be asked to blow up the White House, assassinate Buffalo Bill and steal the Statue of Liberty).

1945: Those filthy American pig-dogs have given our army here a right thrashing and now they are all dead! There are Yanks everywhere! Me and my three comrades are hiding out in the hills. No way will we surrender!

1945 A few months later: Still hiding out. But we he have also been sabotaging and killing like crazy! We must hang on in here! It won't be long before our glorious Japanese army returns and takes back this island from these American cockroaches.

June 1945: Doing loads of guerilla stuff! Strangling! Blowing up! All sorts. And there are bananas everywhere. So we don't go hungry. We can hang on here for months. Years if necessary!

Meanwhile back in the real world: On August 15th the Japanese Emperor announced that Japan had surrendered to the Americans. World War Two was finally over. However, what with not having a daily newspaper (or decent broadband coverage), Hiroo and his pals had no idea this had happened.

1947: We're still holed up in the jungle, sabotaging and killing. Won't our glorious comrades be proud of us when they finally liberate this island?

1948: We have eaten so many bananas that we are starting to look like bananas. Still, it's for a great cause! Every banana we eat takes our glorious country a step closer to winning the war! And we can't complain. We do manage to kill the odd iguana, wild boar or water buffalo. Which make a nice change from bananas.

September 1949: Oh no! Yuichi's done a runner! Maybe all the bananas did send him bananas? But that's no excuse! The cowardly traitor!

After wandering around for six months, Yuichi met some Philippine soldiers who told him the war had been over for five years. 'Oh dear!' he said, 'I better let the others know!'. So he led the soldiers to the spot where he'd last seen Hiroo and left him a note.

March 1950: Found this note from Yuichi at our old campsite this morning...

Dear Hiroo, This might come of something of a surprise, but I thought you ought know that the Second World War actually finished five years ago! Yes, old pal, it's finally safe to come out! Kindest regards, Yuichi BTW ... we lost.

What a load of codswallop! That traitor Yuichi has joined the blinking enemy and now they're trying to trick us into coming out of hiding with their pathetic porkie-pies about the war being over. As if! Me and my two pals have decided to hide in an even thicker part of the jungle.

'Oh dear!' said the Japanese and Philippine authorities. 'That Hiroo's so loyal and so good at hiding. And he's still killing and sabotaging willy-nilly (much to Willy's dismay). Whatever will we do to convince him that we're for real?'

June 1950: Guess what! Those sneaky Americans have flown a Japanese aeroplane over the jungle and dropped letters which are 'supposed' to be from my family, begging me to give up. Along with what are 'supposed' to be recent photographs of them! Do they really think they can fool me? This is just the sort of trick they used to warn us about in guerilla warfare training!

So the letters, which, of course, were totally genuine, had no effect. Next, the Japanese brought Hiroo's brother to the jungle with a really big megaphone and he yelled, 'Yoo hoo, Hiroo! It's me, your brother! The war's been over for yonks. Please come out!'

Would you believe it? Now they've even got an actor who looks just a tinsy little bit like my brother to try and trick me out of here. The snivelling Yankee rats!'

October, 1972: Yesterday we got caught sabotaging and my dear comrade Kozuka was shot dead! Now I am alone in the jungle.

November 1972: Those snivelling rats are bombarding me with fake newspapers containing fake photographs which are supposed to be of Kozuka's funeral back in Japan. Pull the other one, you double-dealing Americans, it's got leeches on! I know for a fact that the war is still on and any day now the glorious Japanese army will be taking this island back from you. All I have to do is to hold out just a bit longer!

In February 1974, almost 30 years after the war had ended, a Japanese university drop-out set off to look for Hiroo, a panda and the Abominable Snowman, in that order (yes, he was even more bonkers than Hiroo!).

1974: Got a bit of a surprise today. This student turned up and said he'd been looking all over for me. Then he told me that the war had finished nearly 30 years ago and that Japan was now really a cool and happening place with washing machines, oven chips and six-lane motorways – whatever they are! Then he asked me to go back to Japan with him. 'Sorry, matey!' I told him. 'Nothing doing. I am a loyal and obedient soldier. I can only do that if I receive orders from my commanding officer. That's what we do in the army, sonny!'

March 10th 1974: That student turned up again today. And guess who he had with him! My old commanding officer, Major Taniguchi. There he was, large as life! You could have knocked me down with a feather!

'Now stop all this silly sabotaging and fighting this minute, Hiroo!' he says to me. 'The war finished 30 blinking years ago. You great patriotic ninny, you! Come home and check out all the great new stuff we've got in Japan now, like floppy discs, Rubik's cubes, post-it notes and chopper bikes.' ... whatever they are?

Then he said, 'Lieutenant Onoda, I order you to lay down your arms!' So being a loyal and obedient soldier, I lay down my sword, my rifle and my hand grenades. And now I have agreed to go home.

When Hiroo got home he wasn't all that impressed with 1970s Japan so he soon went off to Brazil to be a cattle rancher, dividing his time between his cows and teaching Japanese teenagers about living in the wild (which he's apparently quite good at).

Like the **IDEA** of being A SURVIVOR like Hiroo, no matter what the danger? Then try out your tenacity, **INTELLIGENCE** and toughness by taking this **test**...

RIGHT MESS – WRONG ADVICE!

UNFORTUNATE FIXES TO FIND YOURSELF IN

Can you keep a clear head and survive them?

Books, TV and the internet are awash with tips about how to survive all manner of tricky situations from shark attacks to being trapped in burning buildings. However, whatever you do, DON'T follow the survival tips for the following perilous situations or you won't last two minutes! Unfortunately, Peter Peabrain, our calamity-prone survival 'expert' has managed to match the set of tips to the wrong situations. See if you can sort out his mix-up and possibly save your own skin while you're at it. Answers on page 150.

1 If you are walking in the woods and are attacked by grizzly bears

a) Peter says…
Never ever argue with them. Just hand over your wallet, car keys, iPod, or whatever else they want from you.

Always assume they are more than likely carrying weapons such as knives, knuckledusters and guns.

If they ask you for cash, give it to them immediately, otherwise they may drag you to the nearest cash machine and force you to withdraw all your savings.

2 If you are caught in a raging forest fire

b) Peter says...

Stand very still with your hands by your sides.

Avoid making any sudden movements.

Most definitely avoid looking it in the eye as this will only make it twice as fierce.

3 If you are attacked by crocodiles

c) Peter says...

First of all try to communicate with them in a respectful and friendly manner.

Next, establish some sort of relationship with them whilst making sure you give them as little information about yourself as possible.

Do not make it obvious that you are listening to what they

say or are trying to pick up any sort of intelligence that could aid your escape.

4 If you are attacked by a dangerous dog

d) Peter says...

Resist the temptation to take off your clothes, no matter how hot and sticky you feel.

Carefully check your boots for scorpions and spiders.

Regularly snack on fruit, leaves and small insects to keep your energy levels up.

5 If you're set upon by muggers

e) Peter says...

If you are carrying a spear gun, don't hesitate use it! Always aim for their eyes or their gills.

If you do happen to see a school of passing dolphins, shout for help. In the past dolphins have been known to come to the aid of people in this sort of situation.

Get onto dry land as quickly as possible!

6 If you are caught in quicksand

f) Peter says...
Immediately turn off the gas and electricity.
Round up your pets and family.
Get to a higher place such as your bedroom, attic or house roof.

7 If you find yourself trapped in a flooded house

g) Peter says...
Conserve your water supply. In other words, don't drink all the water at once.
Just sip it at regular intervals.
However, don't think you've got to deny yourself a drink when you feel like one. People have actually been found dead of thirst in situations like this even though there is still plenty of water left.

8 If you are trapped in a hotel fire

h) Peter says...
You should speak to it in a normal and calm voice whilst slowly backing away from it.

Carefully study its behaviour, if it makes woofing or moaning sounds this could be an indication that it thinks you are invading its territory.

Another good trick in this situation is to raise your arms above your head to make it think you are bigger than you actually are.

9 If you are attacked by a shark

i) Peter says...

Stub a burning cigarette out on it. Or just sprinkle some salt on it.

If this doesn't work, simply allow it to suck out your blood until it is completely full, then it will leave you alone.

However, if it is holding onto your mouth, ear, nose or private parts, you must immediately seek out a doctor and get them to remove it.

10 If you get lost in the jungle

j) Peter says...

First turn off the air conditioning.

Now cover your head with a wet towel.

Phone reception to find out just how serious the situation is.

11 If kidnappers take you hostage

k) Peter says...

Run away as quickly as you can, they're fast runners, but only over short distances.

If you can't run away just stand on their neck in order to prevent them from opening their massive jaws.

If they do manage to seize hold of you, play dead. If you're lucky they may eventually put you on one side to eat later on.

12 If you're being sucked by a leech

l) Peter says...

Do not run around wildly, plan your escape from it and if your clothes do catch fire whilst doing so, roll around in the undergrowth to put them out.

Do not head for high ground, they always travel faster uphill.

If all else fails, dig a hollow and cover yourself with soil, breathe through cupped hands until it has passed by.

13 If you find yourself stranded under the scorching sun of the sahara desert

m) Peter says...
Get rid of your backpack.
Lay on your back.
Now travel across the sand by rolling your body over and over. Keep going until you reach a safe place.

Answers:
1 h) 2 l) 3 k) 4 b) 5 a) 6 m) 7 f) 8 j) 9 e) 10 d) 11 c) 12 i) 13 g)

With INTELLIGENCE, courage, common sense and experience, it's possible to survive all sorts of dangers. However, sometimes something comes along that even the toughest of the tough don't get through, such as the TERRIBLE DISASTER that took place on...

THE DAY THAT PIGS FLEW AND SHIPS SOARED SKYWARDS

You may have heard of the Great Plague of 1665 and the Great Fire of London that took place in 1666, but have you heard of the Great Storm of 1703?

The second half of November 1703 had been particularly windy with ferocious gales bringing chimneys crashing into the streets and sending roof tiles spinning. But, those winds looked like gentle summer breezes next to the positive humdinger of a hurricane that walloped southern Britain on the night of 26 November 1703! This is what happened on that night to remember.

THE **DAILY POST** 27th November 1703

HORROR HURRICANE FROM HELL BRINGS DEATH AND DESTRUCTION TO BATTERED BRITAIN

GREAT STORM SPECIAL!

Who'd have believed that our green and pleasant land could be so devastated by such a humdinger of a storm? But it has! And here are some of its terrible consequences!

Our weather girl, Gale Storm, reports…

EDDYSTONE AND HIS LIGHTHOUSE VANISH OFF CORNWALL COAST

'Whoosh!' went the lighthouse, along with its creator Henry Winstanley.

Well, Henry, you did say you wanted to experience 'the greatest storm that ever blew under the face of heaven', so you could see how well your building 'stood up to it'. Wish granted!

15,000 KILLED IN SOUTHERN ENGLAND!

Next the maelstrom positively ripped along the southern coast of England, killing a staggering 15,000 people and injuring many thousands more. Such was the chaos caused by the catastrophe that the true figures will never be known. The worst losses were at sea where hundreds of ships were sunk and thousands of our brave sailor lads drowned.

MEN, WOMEN AND CHILDREN 'BLOWN INTO THE AIR'!

Many people, including Daniel Defoe (national treasure and author), watched in astonishment as chickens, sheep

and pigs were blown high into the air. And, even more amazingly, men, women and children were whisked off their feet by the roaring tempest then carried dozens of feet before being dropped back to earth.

Barns, sheds and stables, haystacks were also blasted skywards and thrown around like scraps of paper. A great tidal wave has surged up the Bristol Channel sweeping across fields and drowning more than 15,000 sheep. Tens of thousands more animals have been drowned all over the country.

WINDMILLS BURST INTO FLAMES! No less than 400 windmills have been destroyed by the winds reaching speeds of 120 mph. Some blew down but, quite amazingly, others burned to the ground because the wind made their wood and cloth sails spin so incredibly fast that friction caused them to burst into flames.

NINE HUNDRED HOUSES AND 300,000 TREES DESTROYED! The winds toppled whole rows of houses while churches lost their spires and roofs. All of the lead from the roof of St Paul's Cathedral was folded like 'a roll of parchment'. In Kent the wind has blown sea spray 17 miles inland, coating the grass in so much salt that now the cows won't eat it. It also lifted a ship from the sea and dropped it several dozen metres inland. Everywhere, roof tiles and bricks litter gardens and streets. Some places are eight inches deep in broken roof tiles! The price of roof tiles has now rocketed from 21 shillings a thousand to 120 shillings a thousand! **WHAT A SHOCKER!**

Fortunately, Britain has never seen such a storm since. But you never know, it could happen again. So tie down your chickens...

LIFE in the old days was said to be 'nasty, brutish and short' (and, more than likely, so was your dad). If things like the **GREAT STORM** didn't bring your existence to a sudden, unexpected and PAINFUL END, there was plenty of other stuff around that would. Stuff like fire, violence, famine, accidents, rotten food and diseases, such as the PLAGUE!

SOME UTTERLY DISGUSTING THINGS YOU MIGHT NOT WANT TO KNOW ABOUT THE GREAT PLAGUE OF LONDON 1665

1 When you get the plague you first feel a deathly, icy chill creep through your body and you begin shivering all over. Next you start twitching and jerking. As you twitch, you vomit, feeling an agonising pain sear through your body. You puke until nothing is left to come out but spit and blood then you are seized by a terrible dark depression accompanied by an excruciating headache which gets worse by the second. You now become covered in fist-sized dribbly lumps known as buboes and you quickly go stark raving mad! You also suffer from nose and mouth bleeds, paralysis of your face and neck, constant hiccupping, partial blindness and deafness, sneezing, lisping, stammering and an unquenchable thirst. And then, at last, you die.

2 Doctors visiting plague-sick patients suddenly dropped dead at their bedside.

People chatting to their friends would actually die halfway through a sentence.

3 Some plague victims were so upset at the 'unfairness' of getting the plague that they tried to pass it on to healthy people. A man covered with dribbling sores chased a girl down the street threatening to kiss her. When he caught her she pushed him to the ground but he grabbed her dress, pulled her down with him and kissed her. A few days later she died from the plague.

4 People driven mad by the plague would bash their heads against trees and walls in an attempt to put themselves out of their misery. One crowd of these unfortunates, all screaming and foaming at the mouth, rushed towards a plague pit at Cripplegate in London. On reaching it they threw themselves in, landing amongst the dead bodies and crying out that they were doomed anyway, so they might as well bury themselves and get it over with.

The Cripplegate grave diggers dashed over to some local shepherds and, borrowing their crooks, they attempted to hook out the living victims. They managed to save about half of them but the rest were buried when the next load of bodies arrived and were dumped on top of them.

5 One thing that people thought would protect them from the plague was smoking, which we now know to be fatal. Consequently, men women and children puffed on pipes or chewed disgusting lumps of tobacco known as quids, spitting out the juice whenever they felt like it! School children were actually encouraged to smoke by their teachers. One Eton schoolboy, called Tom Rogers, was actually whipped for not smoking his pipe at breakfast.

6 One of the jobs the plague made necessary was driving a cart around the streets accompanied by an assistant who would ring a bell as they cried, 'Bring out yer dead!' (or 'Bring out your dead!', if they were posh). Quite understandably, most people weren't keen to apply for this job, so the authorities were forced to employ the dregs of society such as burglars, drunkards and pickpockets. These ne'er-do-wells were quite pleased to get the job because they were well paid, and they mainly worked at night. And that meant they could spend their days and their wages boozing. Nor did they seem to mind wearing clothes that were filthy with blood, pus and other, even more disgusting stuff. Probably because they were permanently sozzled!

7 Of course, working so close to all that disease the drivers did catch the plague and some died while driving their carts. When this happened their cart horses might run out of control, stampeding around the streets, scattering plague corpses here there and everywhere until the cart eventually tipped over, dumping its grisly load in the middle of the road. When one driver died, though, his very well-trained horses continued their journey to the plague pit. Then, on arrival, they simply carried on walking and toppled into it, cart, driver and all.

Despite all this death and misery there was at least one person who had a miraculous escape from the miseries associated with the plague...

Saved – by DOGGED determination!

Accompanied by his pet dog, a highland Scottish busker dressed in a kilt regularly walked around seventeenth-century London playing his bagpipes in the hope of getting tips from passers-by (such as, 'Why don't you learn to play the bagpipes?'). However as the plague took more and more victims there were fewer and fewer people about to give him money and he soon began to go hungry. Nevertheless, he battled on, managing to stay alive and to avoid catching the deadly plague.

Then, in September, 1665, when the plague was at its very worst, a friend invited the busker to go for a drink to celebrate them both having survived so far. The Scotsman had a very empty stomach and he also hadn't enjoyed an alcoholic drink for some time, so it's not surprising that, soon after leaving the pub, he collapsed on the pavement, unconscious.

As darkness fell, people living nearby mistook the busker for a plague corpse and brought a body out of their house and laid it next to him. Not long afterwards the plague cart arrived and the driver and his assistant hooked this pair of 'dead bodies' by their belts and dropped them among all the other corpses. The plague cart continued on its way and the still-unconscious busker was gradually buried beneath an ever-increasing pile of dead bodies. However, for the entire time this was happening, his faithful little dog (who had quite sensibly decided not to take part in the booze-up) ran behind the cart barking and whimpering pitifully for its master. Eventually the cart arrived at the plague pit to dump the bodies. It was at this point that the dog's baying and howling became so loud that it woke its master from his drunken sleep. He now fought his way up through the heap of bodies finally arriving the top, looking and feeling absolutely terrible. For some reason known only to himself he put his bagpipes to his lips and began to play. The cart driver and his assistant looked round to see the terrifying sight of the strange figure sitting on top the corpses, eerily lit by their flickering torches. One glance was enough, and an instant later the two of them fled the scene yelling that they had just seen the Devil himself, leaving the Scotsman to dust himself down and make his way home. Dead lucky, or what?

DOGS can be useful, can't they? It's amazing to think that all dogs, including tiny Chihuahuas and gigantic Great Danes, have all been bred from WOLVES. And the one reason for selective breeding, as it's known, is to produce dogs to do a job, whether it be guarding homes, rounding up sheep, helping the police (or stacking shelves in supermarkets). Some dogs have been bred to do very unusual jobs indeed. Here are six of them. However, one of them is made-up. Can you spot it?

THE NORWEGIAN PUFFIN HOUND

Appearance: Small, long thick fur, pointed ears, and nose. Tail curls over back. Reddish brown colour with patches of white but can vary.

Job: The Norwegian Puffin Hound was once used to hunt the rainbow-beaked birds known as puffins (which is probably why they didn't call it the Norwegian Blue-Tit Hound).

Special talents/features: The puffin hound has six toes on each foot, unlike other dogs which only have four (paw things). It used its terrifically talented toes to grasp rocky outcrops and squeeze itself up crevices as it scaled, mountain-climber fashion, the vertical cliffs where the puffins built their nests.

They can also:

a) seal their ears shut by folding them forwards or backwards

b) rotate their legs 90 degrees and hold them out straight from their bodies

c) tilt their heads backwards 180 degrees over their shoulders so that they touch their own backbone (and moon-walk like Michael Jackson)

Nowadays puffin hounds are mainly kept as pets.

THE NEWFOUNDLAND

Appearance: Enormous and hairy. Colour mainly black brown or grey.

And, just like ducks, they have webbed feet! This helps them hugely when they're busy getting on with their **Job:** rescuing shipwrecked sailors or saving the lives of drowning adults and children.

Special talents/ features:

One brave Newfoundland dog saved no less than 92 people when it swam out to their sinking ship, grabbed a rope which they threw to it, then swam back to shore with the rope. The people then pulled themselves to safety along the rope with the Newfoundland swimming alongside just in case they lost their grip (after which, it laid them all out on the beach and gave them mouth-to-mouth resuscitation).

Another Newfoundland dog, whose owners called it 'Hairy Man' (they were very shortsighted), helped save 180 people who were marooned on a rock that was being swamped by mountainous waves. And when Napoleon Bonaparte managed to fall out of his boat whilst escaping from the island of Elba, a fisherman's Newfoundland immediately leapt into the water, grabbed the French Emperor and kept him afloat until he could be rescued (then thrown back when they realized who he was).

Take note! The Newfoundland's passion for saving people from watery graves does have its drawbacks. These brave, powerful (and profoundly thick) dogs are so keen to do their duty that they are unable to distinguish between a real emergency and someone enjoying water-based leisure activities. Consequently, they regularly hurl themselves into rivers, lakes and swimming pools and 'rescue' people who do not actually need, or want, to be rescued! So, don't take your Newfoundland to a swimming gala or your local Aqualand!

Some dogs are talented aren't they? However, according to the first book on our next bonkers book titles list (P 173), they also have a serious problem more normally associated with restless schoolchildren!

THE TURNSPIT DOG

Appearance: Small, like a furry dachshund with very short legs and small ears. Colour: Usually black and tan.

Job: When olden-days folk roasted a joint of meat on a spit above a fire it had to be constantly turned to make sure that it was roasted evenly all over. This was done by 'turnspits'. As a career choice being a turnspit was both tiring and boring with little opportunity for moving on to more rewarding occupations such as IT consultancy, interior design or quantum physics. Consequently the queue for the turnspit vacancies at Ye Olde Jobbe Centre was extremely short. The problem of too many spits and not enough turners was solved by breeding these little dogs which were then bunged into a sort of hamster wheel attached to the spit. The dogs would spend hours running in the wheel while turning the spit and going absolutely nowhere. Because this activity was quite exhausting, most kitchens would have two turnspit dogs. One would turn the spit while the other rested (but most probably didn't go for a walk).

special talents/features Because of their thick fur, short legs and long bodies, turnspit dogs also made excellent draught excluders and their owners would take them to church to keep their tootsies toasty in winter while the vicar droned on interminably. It's said that during one of these sermons the Bishop of Gloucester happened to say the words 'Ezekiel saw the wheel', at which point all the turnspit dogs ran out of the church (but this is probably a shaggy turnspit dog story).

With the introduction of mechanized turnspits there was no longer a use for turnspit dogs so they were allowed to die out. However, there is a turnspit dog in Abergavenny Museum in Wales. He lives in a glass box alongside what looks like a sprig of parsley. His name is Whiskey and he's stuffed (possibly with sage and onion).

THE TENNESSEAN LASSIE

Appearance: Very long fur, medium-size, lightly-built with pointed snout and erect ears. Colour usually brown with white 'collar' around neck and shoulders.

Job: The Tenessean Lassy is one of the bravest and most intelligent dogs known to mankind. They were originally bred to save the lives of the hordes of extremely stupid, freckle-faced, blonde-haired,

American boys who are forever stepping on sleeping grizzly bears, getting trapped in old mine-shafts and falling off cliffs.

Special talents/features: The Lassie is renowned for its courage and resourcefulness. For instance, in the case of the cliff-fall, the Lassie will either: a) climb down to the boy, check him for serious injuries then race to the nearest highway where, ignoring cars driven by ordinary people, it will flag down one driven by a passing doctor whose hobby just happens to be rock-climbing or b) race back to the family farm then, by a series of morse-code style wags of its tail or taps of its paw, will alert the boy's family to the map coordinates of the cliff. To which they will invariably respond, 'Oh no, not again! That's the fifth time he's fallen off it this week!' In the case of the bear, the Lassie will also race back to the farm. Then, after whining frantically and using its paw to sketch out a remarkably lifelike image of an enraged bear in the dirt, it will seize the trousers of the boy's father in his teeth and drag him to the scene of the attack. Here, after rescuing his son, the grinning farmer will make a hilarious quip and the two of them will laugh uproariously. At this point the Lassie will unfailingly bark furiously and wag its tail, indicating that it has understood the joke, including its subtle wordplay.

THE KOREAN JINDO

Appearance: rather like a puffin hound, Colour: white, red fawn, grey, black, black and tan, and brindle (tiger pattern).

Job: The Korean Jindo is the perfect dog for people who like the idea of going into the great outdoors, hunting things, killing them and eating them – but can't be bothered to do the hunting bit! Or, for that matter, the outdoors bit. All you do is say to your faithful Jindo, 'Go out and catch something for tea, Bonzo!' (in Korean, of course). Then, while you sit in front of the telly watching something suitably adventurous, off goes your Jindo, returning some time later with a freshly caught rabbit, pheasant or duck. And if the prey is too heavy for it to carry, for instance if it's a really big deer (hippopotamus or yak), your faithful Jindo trots home to fetch you to help it with the carrying. Or, if you've got more than one Jindo, one of them nips home for you while the others guard the catch (or ring for a taxi).

Special talents/features: The Jindo, unlike other dogs, but just like cats, actually buries its own mess (while the really clever ones actually clear it up with a poop-scoop then drop it in the nearest doggy-doings bin). And that's not all! The multi-talented Jindos are able to recognize over 30,000 different scents (skunk, wild boar, fish and chips, Hugo Boss, you name it!). Which is why the Korean army use them on their military bases where they go around sniffing people just to make sure they aren't enemy infiltrators who have sneaked into the camp, intent on doing something wicked (like stealing all their Jindos!).

Answer: The made-up dog was the Tennessean Lassie. 'Lassie' was actually the name of the dog that originally appeared in the 1943 hit movie LASSIE COME HOME. Lassie was played by a dog called Pal and since then Pal's descendants have acted the part of Lassie in lots more movies. Lassie is actually a type of sheep dog known as a 'Collie'.

TEN MORE BONKERS — BUT TOTALLY TRUE — BOOK TITLES

1) All Dogs Have Attention Deficit Hyper Disorder

2) Excrement in the Late Middle Ages

3) 2009-2014 World Outlook for 60-milligram Containers of Fromage Frais

4) Baboon Metaphysics

5) The Large Sieve and its Applications

6) Strip and Knit with Style

7) Techniques for Corrosion Monitoring

8) A Field Guide to Tattooed Mountain Women and Spoon Boxes of Dagestan

9) How To Avoid Huge Ships

10) Curbside Consultation of the Colon

WHY DO WE SAY ... IT'S RAINING CATS AND DOGS?

We usually only say this when it's raining really, really heavily. In other words, when we're suffering the sort of torrential downpours which, more often than not lead to flooding. Nowadays, we're fortunate enough to have things like man-made gutters, soakaways, drains and river embankments, which lessen the effects of these heavy rainstorms. However, in times-gone-by, cities, towns and villages had no such things. So when it rained really heavily, lanes and alleyways were soon waist-deep with swirling flood waters which swept away everyone and everything in their path. Another thing these places didn't have were sanctuaries for abandoned dogs and cats and as a result the streets were always full of forlorn Fidos and forsaken Felixes. So when it rained really heavily, lots and lots of these stray pets would be caught up in the surging floodwater and drowned. Consequently people would soon be seeing the bodies of the unfortunate creatures floating past, or even through, their houses. 'Well!' they'd exclaim, 'Would you look at that. It's raining cat and dogs!' (and after the storm the streets would be full of poodles).

Here's another sort
of **FLOOD** which you
definitely wouldn't
want to be caught in
– unless, perhaps, if
you were a WASP!

THE GREAT TREACLE TSUNAMI OF 1919

How 21 people met a very sticky end

It was a strangely warm January afternoon in 1919 in the American city of Boston. People at the treacle factory first realized something was wrong when they heard a deep rumbling sound coming from a gigantic, 58-feet high, storage tank containing more than 2 million gallons of treacle. Even more alarmingly, the rumbling was now joined by a sound like that of bullets being fired from a gun. The worried workers looked up to see that the rivets which had previously held the tank together were now snapping like matchsticks. Next, the ground began to shake, there was a huge roar and the massive tank of treacle exploded!

A great spout of the stuff shot out of the shattered container, gushing across the factory yard and out onto the surrounding streets. In the next instant a positive tsunami of treacle was rolling through the neighbourhood, engulfing all who stood in its path. Men, women and children who had first been hurled high into air by the blast of the explosion, now fell back into the treacle and were sucked into the sticky flood, their ears, eyes, mouths and noses immediately filling up with the thick, choking goo, preventing them from seeing, hearing, calling for help, and finally, from breathing. Dogs, cats and horses also were caught up in the flood and the more they struggled to escape from its gooey clutches the more it sucked them in.

Buildings were swept away by the tide of treacle and an elevated railway was toppled by it. Rescuers had their boots sucked from their feet as they rushed into the syrupy swamp to try and pull the victims clear, many of whom had been so completely enveloped in the gluey mess that they were totally unrecognizable as human beings.

Hundreds of rescuers worked through the night doing their best to drag victims from the swamp of syrup. However despite their brave efforts, 21 people, including two children, died in the disaster and another 150 were injured.

Here's the STORY of another sort of flood – but this one was rather smelly!

OH, SCHLITT! — WHAT HAVE YOU GONE AND DONE THIS TIME?

The loo that gushed, when it should have ... flushed!

If you need the loo on a ship, you go just as you would on land. Afterwards, the ship's plumbing system sees to it that all your waste is jettisoned into the sea. However going to the loo on a submerged submarine is a lot trickier! This is because it's not possible to simply open a door, hatch or porthole then blithely release your crud into the briny.

During the Second World War, the German submarines known as U-boats could have up to as many as 70 sailors on board who might spend over two months, deep under the water, without surfacing once. And, unless they happened to be really good at 'holding it', during that time, the crew would produce quite a lot of 'personal waste matter'. The problem was what to do with it all! Storing it in the cramped submarine would not only have taken up precious space but would also have been a health risk, not to mention really pongy!

Somehow the waste had to be flushed into the sea without the sea simultaneously flushing back into the sub. German submarine designers solved this problem by constructing a special, high-pressure U-boat loo. However, it was incredibly complicated to use and submariners needed advanced 'potty-training' to learn how to operate the complex series of valves that sent waste into an airlock where it was jettisoned into the sea by a blast of compressed air.

On 14 April 1945 a German U-boat was 200 feet under the North Sea just outside the Scottish port of Peterhead when its commander, Captain Schlitt, realized that he needed to pay an urgent visit to his ship's new superloo. However, when he'd finished, not being familiar with the 'in and outs' of the device and being too embarrassed to ask for help, he had a go at operating it himself. This wasn't a good idea!

Instead of flushing, the superloo began gushing and in the next instant Captain Schlitt found himself up to his neck in seawater and raw sewage. He immediately leapt out of the loo compartment, closely followed by the tons of seawater which were now pouring into his ship. The seawater soon found its way into the battery compartment where, on mixing with battery acid, it produced clouds of deadly chlorine gas.

There was only one thing for it! If the crew wasn't to suffer an agonising death, the sub would have to surface straight away. But it really wasn't Captain Schlitt's day. As his sub popped up out of the North Sea it was spotted by the crew of a British warplane who immediately dropped a bomb on it. Captain Schlitt and his crew now abandoned ship, leaving their stricken sub to sink to the bottom of the ocean. Some time later they were later picked up and taken to a British prisoner of war camp where, Captain Schlitt was no doubt relieved to discover, the toilets were incredibly straightforward to use!

After their ordeal in the sea CAPTAIN SCHLITT and his soaking wet crew might well have benefitted from trying out our final...

Something BONKERS to do on a boring Sunday afternoon

Number four

Turn yourself into an amazing ... HUMAN RADIATOR!

This awesome activity is 'enjoyed' by the Buddhist monks who live in the snow-covered mountains of Tibet. These monks do a lot of meditating. In other words, they spend long periods of time sitting around thinking really deep thoughts whilst in an extra-relaxed frame of mind. One of the types of meditation they learn to do is called tumo, which is basically a test of whether or not they've got what it takes to become a fully fledged monk, finally achieving such fantastic powers of mind-over-matter that they could actually turn the telly on and off, simply by thinking it – well not quite (and, more to the point, most Tibetan monks don't watch telly). Of course you'll need quite a lot of determination to get to grips with your tumo. However, once you do, you'll be able to amaze your friends and rellies with this astonishing trick. And, as you'll soon see, you're never likely to ever be accused of being a 'big wet blanket'! If you survive the training!

What you need:

One sheet - YES, that's all!

What to do:

1 Take your sheet and climb to a frozen lake, preferably high in the snowy Himalayan Mountains. If you can't manage the Himalayas, you could always go to the English Lake District or a local pond on a bitterly cold, snowy December evening. The main thing is that it must be somewhere where the temperatures are way below freezing. And, to make sure they're extra way below freezing, you must do this at night.

2 Hang around for ten minutes or so until you're thoroughly 'chilled out'.

3 Feeling cold? Don't worry, quite soon this will seem like a summer afternoon!

4 Now take off all your clothes. Yes, all of them!

5 Next, sit down in the snow. By the way, you should be into some serious industrial-strength meditating by this point. And the main thing you should be doing is trying to convince yourself that you are NOT cold!

6 Got yourself well focused on lots of TOASTY WARM thoughts? Good! It's finally time to do the stuff with your sheet! Make a hole in the ice of the lake or pond. Dip your sheet in the water until it's completely saturated.

7 Now, this next bit may come as a bit of a shock, both mentally and physically! What you must do next is to wrap your soaking-wet sheet around your body. Yes, BRRRRR to the power of 100!

And now comes the really tricky bit.

8 Intensify your trance-like, meditative state. What do you mean, your teeth won't stop chattering? Tell them to shut up! Now, using all your powers of concentration and determination you must persuade your shivering body to produce enough heat to actually dry out the soaking-wet sheet which is wrapped around you. That's assuming that your body has any heat left in it and that you haven't actually turned into a human popsicle.

Yes, quite a challenge, isn't it? But, believe it or not bit-by-bit, the Tibetan monks actually manage to dry out their sheet completely.

Inspired? Determined to dry your sheet?

9 Go for it then! And remember, clammy, or merely damp, won't do! We're talking crisp and bone-dry like it's been in the tumble drier!

10 You've done it? Congratulations! 'Yippee!' you may now cry. 'I've cracked it! Everyone back to the monastery/my house/hospital for hot buttered yak/steaming cocoa/intensive care.'

Don't be silly. This is merely round one!

11 You must now soak your sheet and once more use your body heat to dry it out again! Then again!

And so it continues. If the monks are going to pass the test, thus achieving their much coveted, Extremely Daft Things To Do Up A Mountain – Idiot Level One badge, they must dry out their sheet at least three times. And if they don't manage that, they are considered to have failed (and also considered to be 'rather wet'). But three sheets is nothing to some of these young hotshots! It's said that some of the really keen ones manage to dry out as many as 40 sheets, in just one night!

Once they've passed the test the monks become known as respas (Tibetan for 'convector heater'), and from that day on they either walk around completely starkers or simply wear a single cotton garment all year round (thus saving a fortune in central-heating bills and thermal undies).

The **Tibetan monks** call the meditation in which they fix their MIND firmly on one thing, such as drying sheets with their body heat, joggom. The world's languages are full of **weird and wonderful** words like joggom. Discover a few of them by trying this...

BONKERS FOREIGN WORDS QUIZ

1 Uitwaaien
a) German for 'Way Out'
b) Dutch for 'walking in windy weather for fun'
c) Albanian for the slurping noise someone makes when
they climb out of a mud bath

2 Igunaujannguaq
a) Swahili for spicy iguana stew
b) Inuit for a game which involves pretending to be a
frozen walrus carcase
c) Mandarin Chinese for the noise loose change makes in
your pocket when you run

3 Pampiervampier
a) French for a bloodsucking fireman
b) Afrikaans for a stapler
c) Italian for giving a room a makeover by decorating it
with really snazzy wallpaper

4 Fryassistent
a) Belgian for someone who works in a fast food outlet
b) Norwegian for someone who persistently hogs the fire by
standing in front of it to warm their bottom
c) Danish for a lighthouse keeper's mate

5 Nakhur

a) Turkish for tiring someone out by making them spend all day working in a kebab shop

b) Persian for a camel that won't give milk until her nostrils have been tickled

c) Ancient Latin for someone who drives their chariot in the nude

6 Rejam

a) Malaysian for pressing someone's face in mud until they die

b) the Old English word for two horses and carts becoming wedged in a narrow lane for the second time in one day

c) French for the spreading of an extra layer of fruit preserve on your toast

7 Tingo

a) Australian Aborigine for a game involving random numbers and lots of shouting

b) Spanish for the sensation which passes along a bullfighter's spine just before he is tossed into the air

c) the Easter Island word for someone who keeps borrowing objects from a friend's house until they have nothing left

Answers: 1b 2b 3b 4c 5b 6a 7c

NOW,
IT'S TIME
FOR SOME
MORE...

BONKERS but totally true magazine titles

DENTAL GLOVE UPDATE

HAIR GROWERS NEWS

EUROPEAN SANDWICH AND SNACK NEWS

HOT DIP GALVANISING

COIL WINDING INTERNATIONAL

MODERN FERRET

CAT FISH INSIDER

BISON WORLD

That last magazine would probably not exist if certain bonkers people in North America, including the President himself, had had their way during the nineteenth century. Nor would the bison!

COMPLETELY BONKERS

And then there were NONE (well, almost)

Nowadays everyone's worried about such rare and wonderful creatures as gorillas, cheetahs, pandas, dolphins, polite children, hippos and rhinos becoming extinct. However, just over a hundred years ago, things were very different. Most people didn't give a dodo's if the last ever white-footed rabbit rat or South African quagga bit the dust. And, in North America, quite unbelievably, thousands of people were quite deliberately doing their very best to wipe out an entire species!

The Bison, or if you want its scientific Latin name, Bison, bison, bison, (yes, so good they named it thrice!) is that huge prehistoric-looking, ox-like creature which looks a very old and tatty walking carpet. Bull bison can grow six feet tall, ten feet long and weigh more than a ton, and their thunderous bellowing can be heard over a mile away.

In the 1850s there were 75 million of these magnificent animals wandering the great grassy prairies of the Wild West. Herds of them, often as enormous as 25 miles wide and 50 miles long, wandered the grassy plains of the North American continent, chewing grass, making baby bison and occasionally having tense stand-offs with wolves and grizzly bears. So huge were these herds that if you stood in one spot watching one pass by, you would see nothing but a vast sea of bison stretching from horizon to horizon. And, even more amazingly, you would be watching it for five days and nights before the very last bison in the herd had trotted past you. Now comes the shock.

By 1902 the total number of these amazing animals left alive in the wild in all of North America was an astonishing 23! How ever did this happen? Read on … and be appalled!

At first the only humans who bothered the bison were the Native American Plains Indians who killed about 2 million every year. As the bison produced 6 million calves a year, this was hardly likely to endanger their survival.

The waste-not/want-not Indians didn't squander a single bit of the bison.

HORNS: BUTTONS, LADLES AND SPOONS

BONES: PAINT BRUSH HANDLES, KNIVES AND SEWING NEEDLES

RIBS: CHILDREN'S SLEDGES

MUSCLES: BOW STRINGS AND THREAD

FAT: CANDLES

TAIL: FLYSWATTER

SKIN: TENTS, DRUMS, SHOES, CLOTHES AND BEDDING

BRAIN: TANNING ACID *

TONGUE: (ROUGH SIDE) HAIRBRUSHES

HOOVES: RATTLES AND GLUE

STOMACH: SOUP KETTLE HEATED BY DROPPING A RED HOT STONE INTO IT

DUNG: FIRES

MEAT: FOOD

* (NO, NOT GOING-BROWN-IN-THE-SUN-TANNING, 'TREATING LEATHER')

But then the white settlers came along and everything changed. The European invaders of North America had quite a few reasons for wanting to wipe out the bison but their main one was greed. Not because they actually wanted to eat every single bison in the USA, which would have been quiet an achievement (even for Americans). No, it was because they wanted the land which the Indians had lived on for thousands of years. And the best way to do that was to destroy the Indians' source of food, heat, light and shelter and wipe out their traditional nomadic way of life. So they set about bison slaughtering on an industrial scale.

The mass extermination began in earnest in the 1870s with huge expeditions, consisting of sharpshooters, bison skinners, cooks, horses, wagons, blacksmiths and gun cleaners setting off for the prairies. One bison hunter could kill a hundred bison at one go. And some of them, like Buffalo Bill, singlehandedly slaughtered tens of thousands in just a few years. And, after they'd been killed, all that was taken from the bison were their skins and their tongues. Their huge bodies were just left to rot. Soon the great plains were littered with millions and millions of stinking bison corpses. Photographers of the era made pictures of mountains of bison skulls as a high as a two storey house.

And so it went on for year after year, with bison shooting becoming a fashionable sport for the rich and privileged, who just sat in trains and picked the poor beasts off without even leaving their comfy carriage seat. And if they weren't a good shot, that didn't matter either. They simply had a live bison tied up in front of them so that they could 'heroically' blast it to pieces. When an attempt was made to put a limit on the slaughter, the President of America himself, determined to see every last living bison exterminated, made sure that no such thing happened. And then, in the 1880s the American government sent out an expedition to find out just how many bison were left. However, after wandering the plains for weeks, they were unable to find a single living bison!

But it wasn't all bad news. During the great hunts a few individuals, determined to save the bison from extinction, caught bison calves then hid them away on their ranches. And, as people finally started to wake up to the idea of conservation, it was those bison which were used to breed new herds which would eventually be reintroduced into the wild. Consequently, and thankfully, there are now about 350,000 bison in North America, some in the wild and some captive. But the only bison which have remained in the wild continuously are descended from the 23 mentioned earlier, who managed to survive the great slaughter by hiding out in a remote valley. That herd now numbers over 3,000. So, it would seem there's hope yet for those rhinos, gorillas, dolphins and polite children.

EVERYONE knows that a group of bison is called a **herd**. But do you know the proper names for other GROUPS OF ANIMALS? Take this test and find out!

COLLECTIVE NOUNS QUIZ

1 Ferrets
a) a trouserful b) a stink c) a busyness

2 Chimpanzees
a) a tea party b) a troop c) a cartload

3 Cheetahs
a) a sprint b) a coalition c) a spotting

4 Baboons
a) a tribe b) a racket c) a threat

5 Penguins
a) a waddle b) a huddle c) a flap

6 Butterflies
a) a flutter b) a rabble c) a cloud

7 Giraffes

a) a forest b) a tower c) a wobble

8 Otters

a) a bundle b) a romp c) a skelter

9 Zebra

a) a barcode b) a crossing c) a zeal

10 Magpies

a) a tiding b) a posse c) a chatter

11 Hamsters

a) a horde b) a whirl c) a cluster

12 Frogs

a) an army b) a greening c) a hopscotch

Answers: 1c 2c 3b 4a 5b 6b 7b 8b 9c 10a 11a 12a

SIX BRILLIANT, BUT BONKERS, FROGS AND ONE TOAD ... THAT ISN'T A TOAD!

1 The paradoxical frog: A grown-up paradoxical frog is only about 6 cm long. However, its tadpoles are over 25 cm long. Which is like a human baby being four times bigger than its parents. Then shrinking as it, er, grows up?

2 The marsupial frog: A marsupial frog's partner catches her eggs as she lays them. Then, after popping them in a little pouch on her back, he fertilizes them. The tadpoles which hatch from the eggs remain in the pouch until they've turned into frogs. At this point their mum opens the pouch with her toes and drops them in the water (then tells them to hop it).

3 The horror frog: When they feel threatened horror frogs actually break their own bones to produce instant claws! They do this by flexing a muscle in their toes which causes the bone to break. The resulting sharp spikes cut through the frog's toe pad giving it instant claws. People who hunt the horror frogs for food in the African country of Cameroon use spears to kill them so that they aren't hurt by their lethal claws.

4 Horned toad: Horned toads can squirt blood from their eyes when they think they're are being threatened (or just feel like showing off). NB This one's a cheat really because horned toads are lizards (and if you're confused, think how the lizard feels).

5 The glass frog: The glass frog is so transparent that it's possible to see all its internal organs quite clearly (unlike its cousin the tinted glass frog).

6 Poison dart frogs are incredibly brightly coloured and vary from slightly poisonous to the totally lethal one-lick-and-you're-a-gonner variety! South American Indian tribes barbecue them in order to extract their poison which they then smear on the tips of their darts (which are now banned in pubs everywhere).

7 Goliath frogs are the biggest frogs in the World. They can grow up to 33 cm long and weigh up to 3 kg. They eat scorpions, insects and smaller frogs. They can't croak but have really good hearing (and are really good at sign language).

Here's a man who was **BONKERS** about FROGS, and lots of other animals!

FRANK BUCKLAND (1826–1888)

Frank Buckland was a naturalist, a writer and Inspector of Salmon Fisheries. He was fanatical about cooking and eating whatever little creatures took his fancy. When he was a little boy he rustled up all sorts of scrumptious treats including squirrel pie, mice cooked in batter and slug soup (hmmm ... slug soup!) Frank also used to like to carry an assortment of living creatures around in his pockets. One day he met a man who kept pet storks and immediately apologized to him for not having any frogs on him to feed to the storks (should think so too, how thoughtless of him!). However, a moment later he said that he did just happen to have a matchbox in his pocket which was 'full of toads, about the size of little beans'. So the storks weren't disappointed after all (unlike the toads).

Frank's pets included a chameleon, an eagle, a jackal and a bear named after the ancient Assyrian king, Tiglath-Pileser. He also had a parrot which spent most of its time at an open window shouting for taxis. One day a fishmonger sent Frank a message to say he had a very big sturgeon which might be of interest to him and that he was welcome to borrow it, adding that the gigantic fish must be back in his shop by ten the next morning. Frank took the fishmonger up on his offer but as he was manoeuvring the nine-foot-long monster down some stone steps in his house, the rope holding it slipped from his grasp and the gigantic creature went bouncing down the stairs, crashed through the kitchen door and slid across the floor, finally coming to rest under the table. The gruesome sea monster's spectacular entrance caused Frank's maid to faint, his cook to have a fit of the screaming hab-dabs, his pet monkeys to go mad with terror and his talking parrot to be struck dumb for ever more (much to the relief of the taxi drivers).

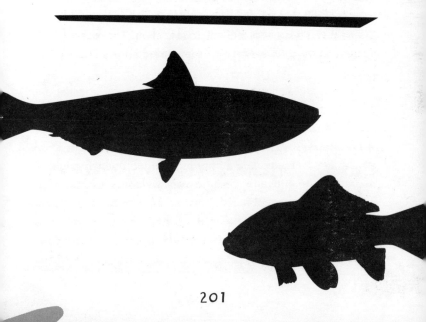

One day a woman visiting Frank's home fell downstairs after tripping over something large and soft in the darkness. It turned out to be a hippopotamus and, as Frank picked the woman up, he said, 'Do be more careful. Hippopotamuses don't grow on trees you know!' (Thereby demonstrating his awesome knowledge of the animal kingdom.)

If someone from EAST LONDON had told Frank they were going to cross a **frog** and **toad**, he may well have assumed they were going to mate the two amphibians (perhaps to produce a FROAD, or a TROG?). But what they would have meant was that they were going to cross the road. This is an example of rhyming slang spoken by the Londoners known as **COCKNEYS**. No one's entirely sure how the rhyming slang developed. However, it's thought that it may have had something to do with criminals using words and phrases that rhymed with the word they meant to use in order to prevent police spies from knowing what they were planning. Take a 'butchers' (butcher's hook = LOOK) then use your 'loaf' (loaf of bread = head) to work out the answers to this...

Cockney RHYMING slang quiz

1 Queen	a) Talk
2 Basil Fawlty	b) Flares
3 Rabbit and Pork	c) Eyes
4 Dustbin Lid	d) Mouth
5 Lionel Blares	e) Curry
6 Mince Pies	f) Sun
7 Plates of Meat	g) Kid
8 Bees and Honey	h) Balti
9 Biscuit and Cheese	i) Baked Bean
10 Bacon and Eggs	j) Money
11 Tom and Dick	k) Sick
12 Ruby Murray	l) Feet
13 North and South	m) Knees
14 Currant Bun	n) Legs

ANSWERS: 1i) 2h) 3a) 4g) 5b) 6c) 7l) 8j) 9m) 10n) 11k) 12e) 13d) 14f)

LAST WORD

As you have now probably worked out, the world we live in is a very amazing, totally intriguing and constantly surprising place. Don't forget what that big brain box Thomas Edison said,

'We only know one millionth of one percent about everything!'

And the trick to discovering all the fascinating undiscovered stuff about our planet and its inhabitants is to never take anything for granted, especially if it comes from the mouth of a TV presenter or similar nitwit who assumes you only have one brain cell. So be constantly curious whilst asking yourself questions like...

WHY are carrots orange?

WHAT animal has killed more people than any other in the history of the world?

WHY are barnacle geese called barnacle geese?

HOW was basketball invented?

HOW many willies has an earwig got?

WHAT animal did Victorian sweeps use to clean chimneys with?

Plus about a billion more questions like that and you'll soon discover that every day is a thrilling adventure where you, the number-one amazing factoid sleuth and seeker after truths which are stranger than fiction are engaged, constantly pitting your wits as you unravel the secrets of the great mystery tale known as life on earth.

OUT NOW→